THE WISCON CHRONICLES
VOL. 5

The WisCon Chronicles

VOLUME 5

Writing and Racial Identity

Edited by
Nisi Shawl

AQUEDUCT PRESS | SEATTLE

Aqueduct Press
PO Box 95787
Seattle WA 99145-2787
www.aqueductpress.com

The WisCon Chronicles, Volume 5
Writing and Racial Identity

ISBN: 978-1-933500-73-7

9 8 7 6 5 4 3 2 1

Cover illustration: "Thought Process," by permission of artist,
James Ng

James Tiptree, Jr. Award art (p. 63) courtesy of Freddie Baer
The text typeface is Cambria, designed by Jelle Bosma with Steve
Matteson and Robin Nicholas

Supported by a grant from the Society for the Furtherance &
Study of Fantasy & Science Fiction [SF3]

Printed in the United States of America
by Applied Digital Imaging, Bellingham, WA

CONTENTS

Introduction

by Nisi Shawl

Some time in January of 2011 I wrote to a friend: "I feel like I am floating in an alternate universe of silver goggles and artificial wombs and look there's Emily Dickinson smoking a cigar." I was deep inside the process of editing *The WisCon Chronicles, Vol. 5: Writing and Racial Identity*, surrounded by all those elements and more—a delightful place. "It will be nice when other people get to read this book," I added.

It is.

There was never a doubt in my mind as to the theme of this fifth volume of the WisCon Chronicles. Almost as soon as Timmi Duchamp asked me to edit it, I knew. "Writing and racial identity," I stated firmly, aloud. It seemed to me a thoroughly WisConsinese topic, one that anyone who attended this famed feminist science fiction convention would be able to address.

Imagine my surprise upon learning that I was mistaken and that many, many people I approached about contributing were hesitant to do so. Some refused me outright. Mostly (but not exclusively) it was white people who found themselves reluctant to discuss the intersection of writing and racial identity.

Maybe I oughtn't to have felt so puzzled; worry over looking stupid and getting this stuff wrong is alive and well thanks to various internet "Fails." (A capital-F Fail is an error-precipitated online conversation about race, gender, or some other common pretext for marginalization.) The concern over coming across as a fool is rational; plenty of us did get it wrong and looked totally stupid in one recent Fail or another. I'm glad, though, that authors of all races had enough to say on the subject that seemed intelligent enough to me to make a whole book. Because the racial identity of WisCon itself has changed. Since iv ∫ Nisi Shawl

WisCon 23 in 1999 — when the POC-in-genre advocacy organization Carl Brandon Society was founded — WisCon attendance by POC has increased tenfold. And eleven years later WisCon 34 played a crucial part in that change, as detailed in the essay immediately following this introduction.

I think we have to talk about that. I *want* to talk about it. I have loved hearing what other people say on the subject.

I'm neither the mother nor the father of anything in this book. But because I've assisted at their births I have a deeply intimate relationship with each and every one of these texts and images. I want you to love them all, yet I know you'll have favorites. Read them and look at them, then tell me which you think is the best.

I'll offer you only one superlative: MJ Hardman's minim opus, "The Russ Categories," has got to be the hardest-won essay in this book. For years MJ has taught a course on applying the lessons of Joanna Russ's *How to Suppress Women's Writing* to the accomplishments of other suppressed groups. With colleague Anita Taylor she has been making of it an interactive online learning experience. I asked her to contribute a condensed version. Right before her deadline she had what's technically known as a "bilateral pulmonary embolic shower." Hundreds of blood clots formed in her lungs. One is enough to kill a person.

MJ apologized from her hospital bed for missing her deadline. A few weeks later, when still a "shut-in" tied to an oxygen tank, she submitted her essay. It is provocative, sweeping, humorous, magnificent. It may well be the book's heart.

If "The Russ Categories" is *Wcc5*'s heart, the multiple interviews Eileen Gunn solicited, compiled, and edited form its well-articulated exoskeleton. A literary armature, the six questions answered in "Racial Identity and Writing: A Dozen Writers and Thinkers Reflect" divide the book into thematic sections and give it a coherent shape. I hope. At any rate, Eileen's respondents are enlightening in their very contradictions. Entertaining, too.

Editing this book has been a joy. My thanks to its many contributors; to Timmi, Kath, and Tom, who have made Aqueduct Press not just possible but real; to SF3, whose grant has made *The WisCon Chronicles, Vol. 5: Writing and Racial Identity* more affordable for you; to Kate Nepveu and the Con or Bust donors, who made the presence of fen of color at

WisCon 34 a force to be reckoned with; and to my ancestors, who made me. I believe this book also owes much to Exu, Afro-diasporic deity of intersectionality; and to his mother, Oshun, goddess of love, wealth, beauty, culture, and transformation, for whom the number five is sacred.

A Short History of Con or Bust

by Kate Nepveu

Con or Bust raises funds to assist people of color to attend WisCon and other science fiction and fantasy conventions committed to increasing racial diversity and understanding in fandom and the field generally. It helped nine people of color attend WisCon in 2009, and thirteen in 2010, as well as helping two publishers of a diversity-focused small press attend WorldCon in 2009. After Con or Bust's first year, the Carl Brandon Society assumed management of the fund, allowing it to become an ongoing project.

Origin

Con or Bust began as a response to RaceFail09, a months-long on-line discussion that was initially about cultural appropriation and racial stereotypes in writing and eventually involved a number of professional authors and editors in science fiction and fantasy behaving in hurtful and harmful ways. I think the most useful summary is this themed one by Ann Somerville at <http://logophilos.net/racefail.html>; links to others of varying detail can be found at <http://wistfuljane.livejournal. com/218945.html>.

I had been going to cons since 1997, and participating in online fan communities a few years before that, and—like many other people—I was deeply hurt, angered, and alienated by the behavior of prominent members of this community, some of whom I had considered friends. Though RaceFail09 strained or broke many relationships, it created others. And in early March 2009, when some fans of color expressed the desire to attend WisCon and meet each other in person, they and others in the conversation, including myself, came up with the idea of a fundraiser to help that happen.

The goal of Con or Bust was to help fans of color attend WisCon, where they would be their own awesome selves. It wasn't a scholarship, it wasn't restricted by either fan or pro status, and there was no requirement that people be on programming or network or anything of the kind (indeed, all requests for assistance were and are confidential). We simply felt that it would be a good thing if there were more fans of color at WisCon and wanted to help that happen.

Fundraising and Assistance

Elizabeth McClellan and I ran an auction on LiveJournal through mid-April 2009. People offered a wide variety of auction items, such as a cameo appearance in a novel; custom-made jewelry or clothing and other craft items; story critiques; baked goods; and, of course, lots and lots of books. The items receiving the highest bids were a seed account at Dreamwidth (a journal service then planning its open-beta launch), and a custom-written short story by Daniel Abraham. We also had two other significant types of contributions: first, transferred memberships to WisCon, which WisCon 33 co-chairs Debbie Notkin and Jim Hudson helped me manage; and second, help with PayPal's restrictions on receiving money, including Deb Stone's donation of transaction fees, and use of her account to accept donations via credit card.

The 2009 fundraiser raised $5,898.14 and helped nine fans attend WisCon 33. Nine people isn't a lot in an absolute sense, but it isn't nothing either, considered against WisCon's thousand-person membership cap. Also, later that year, Con or Bust helped two people of color attend WorldCon as representatives of a small press focused on diversity.

Because Con or Bust's auction started so late relative to the May weekend on which WisCon takes place, we weren't able to allocate all the donations we collected to potential attendees. We were left with a surplus of funds, which we donated to the Carl Brandon Society. (As the comment about PayPal may have suggested, I was running this fundraiser out of my personal bank account, which I was only willing to do on a very limited basis.) The CBS then agreed manage Con or Bust's funds and apply the donation to Con or Bust's ongoing efforts. Since the CBS is a 501(c)(3) organization, this also allowed future donations to Con or Bust to be tax-deductible to the extent permitted under U.S. law.

In 2010, the auction ran for two and a half weeks in February and March. We had similar kinds of things offered, but considerably more people offering them. The items receiving the highest bids were a signed, personalized first edition hardcover of Neil Gaiman's *Anansi Boys* and a podfic recording of an epic-length (no word limit) fanfic story of the winner's choosing.

We raised $6,183.89 and helped thirteen people attend WisCon 34. Unfortunately, we did not have the funds to help everyone who requested assistance, so we will be trying to raise more money in 2011.

WisCon 34 Gathering

In 2010, Con or Bust also ran a Characters of Color Fantasy Faceoff at the Gathering, with the final rounds at the Carl Brandon Society's party. This was a light-hearted bracket-style challenge meant to give people the opportunity to promote their favorite characters of color and make silly arguments about who was more awesome. In the end, Zoe Washburn from *Firefly* defeated Yeine from N.K. Jemisin's *The Hundred Thousand Kingdoms* to win the entire Faceoff. The full bracket results can be found at <http://community.livejournal.com/con_or_bust/55591.html>.

This event came about almost entirely because of people other than me—I've never actually been to WisCon, and so it was only Jackie Lee's encouragement that prompted me to look into doing something at the Gathering. Elizabeth McClellan and Mikki Kendall not only volunteered at WisCon but handled the earlier collection of character nominations, while Andy Best, Sterling Novak, and Saira Ali helped with the voting.

Feedback

As I said, I've yet to attend WisCon myself. But I've seen a number of people say that they noticed more fans of color at WisCon 33 and 34. Con or Bust can't take credit for all of that increase, but I believe it did contribute, since many of those assisted by Con or Bust said that they wouldn't have been able to attend otherwise. This increased membership also supports and is supported by at-con efforts of fans of color to connect with and support each other, such as informal get-togethers and a safe space for people of color. And, on a more individual scale, a number of those assisted have told me that they had a great time and were very glad to have gone, which is Con or Bust's most basic goal.

Future Plans

Con or Bust's future plans are pretty simple: spread the word that assistance is available more widely, raise more money, and help more fans of color attend WisCon and, hopefully, other cons with a commitment to diversity. We're planning to get a logo designed so that we can sell T-shirts and such year-round, and will continue to work on making the yearly auction bigger, more diverse, and even more full of terrific items. And, on a personal note, one of these years I hope to make it to WisCon myself and see the results of so many people's hard work and good will in person.

Remarks from Con or Bust Beneficiaries

(Recipients of Con or Bust grants are anonymous.)

Recipient One: Last year I was lucky enough to be a Con or Bust benefi-
ciary. This deeply impacted my research by allowing me to be mentored
by Andrea Hairston, with whom I now email back and forth, and Nisi
Shawl, whose work as an Afrocentric writer and blogger has deeply impacted my work on global citizens' movements.

Attending WisCon under the auspices of the Carl Brandon Society,
Con or Bust's administrator, was also especially useful to me as a fan of
color. I met many of the authors and bloggers of color I had been inter-
acting with online for the last several years. This encounter felt more
like a homecoming than anything else.

Finally, when attending WisCon I had the opportunity to hear authors like N.K. Jemisin talk about her work as an activist, Nisi Shawl reflect on authors writing as allies, and Mary Anne Mohanraj speak on
motherhood, eroticism, and her own evolution as an author. I also became a juror for the CBS Parallax Award, which has been an amazing
experience.

⊷⊜⊜⊷

Recipient Two: I attended WisCon for the first time last year, and it was
an amazing experience. I met authors whose work I love, spoke with
other fans and writers of color, discussed issues that matter deeply to
me, participated on my first panel, and even gave a reading of my own. I
cannot begin to express how all that helped me realize there is, indeed,
a place for me and for my work, or how it encouraged me to keep speaking about diversity and social justice both within the realm of speculative literature and outside it. I've written essays and been interviewed
since then, not to mention producing more of my own fiction.

But I wouldn't have been able to take part in the WisCon experience without the financial support Con or Bust provided me. Because it covered my hotel and plane costs and included a stipend for food, I didn't have to worry about whether or not I could afford the trip. Instead, I could concentrate on the things that mattered: sharing my voice, taking part in the conversation, furthering my own dream of seeing Indian YA fantasy in print. For that, I'm more grateful than I can say.

⇥▬◉◖▬⇤

Recipient Three: Getting the money to attend WisCon was an unexpected boon and made me grateful. In a way I also felt a bit guilty about receiving it since I did have a job, and then a smattering of angry stopped by for a visit. What brought anger to my door? Thinking how I have a job and live in this supposed great land, but I still needed aid to get to do something fun and couldn't do it on my own.

Overall, I'm glad I went, glad I got the funding, and hope I can return the favor in the near future so someone else can get a taste of WisCon.

My First WisCon

by Tanya C. DePass

> *Disclaimer*—I wrote this piece about four months
> post WisCon 34, so if I misspeak about anything I
> did or said, apologies up front. Also any stories and
> references to WisCon 33 are via conversations with
> friends, and LiveJournal and other postings about the
> fail there as well as the good times. So again, if I've
> misremembered anything passed along the inter-
> webs about the 2009 WisCon, I ask your forgiveness
> in piecing things together via a memory that's
> somewhat shot as well as year-old stories of a WisCon
> past that I didn't attend.

So, WisCon 34 was my first experience attending a sci-fi convention with a target audience of feminists. I really didn't know what to expect, since I'm not a big con-goer in recent years. I was nervous due to several factors. For one thing, as far as WisCon attendees I only knew the other three folks in the car that I was coming with. Also, I had no clue how big WisCon was, and I was worried about the drive there. Since I'd never actually driven out-of-state before and since there was no one else in the car that could take over I was a bundle of nerves until we got to the con hotel. There was also the specter of RaceFail09 hanging over my head and coloring my expectations of what I'd take away from the con.

I worried about being there as a person of color (POC), as well as a newbie, since these kinds of things can be intimidating the first time around, and most of all I worried/wondered what exactly I'd do since there was so much going on, with sessions I was interested in often over-lapping each other. Once I was checked in, I had just enough time to get to Tempest Bradford's Dinner for Fans of Color. It was a fun start to the evening, where I got to meet some of the authors I'd recently discovered, as well as other POC in attendance, and most importantly I had a chance to decompress before facing the con itself. That brought out some mild social anxiety, especially after walking into a crowded hotel lobby during the beginning of the dinner break. That anxiety was eased by running into a couple of folks who I knew but hadn't realized were going to be at WisCon, so that helped out with the omg-too-many-people-flee instinct that threatened to consume me before I hit the POC dinner.

Once the dinner was over, I hung about the hotel for a bit and then I hit up the LiveJournal party since there were LJ folks I knew I wanted to see. I was exhausted by the time 11:00 came and my memory is of course not serving me well as I write this, but I know Day One was short but sweet. I remember being annoyed because I'd really wanted to get to the "How Did All the Thin White People Take Over Space?" panel. That session was on bodies in sci-fi, an issue I'm really interested in due to my own roundish physique. I missed it, though. Ah, well, there's always next year, and the write-up that exists in cyber-space. Somewhere in the melée before calling it a night, I picked up my badge, a few goodies, and most importantly a program booklet that I could carry about with me.

Day Two was full of wow: people, sessions—what to do first?! Luckily that problem was solved when I ran into folks going to the Farmers Market, and in between tasty treats for the day and conversation with seasoned con-goers I started to feel a bit more at ease with being away from home and somewhat out of my element. I popped over to the "Politics of Steampunk" panel, but it didn't do too much for me. I left before it ended and snuck into a session I'd really had my eyes on, "Race Basics," which I'd hoped would touch on RaceFail and more importantly the expectation that POC will educate non-POC on racial issues, plus why we aren't just running around angry for no good reason. The panel was so much fun, done in a game show style that provided a much needed break from the weight of serious panels earlier in the day. I laughed so much at the questions and audience responses I needed water and a stretch afterward.

I wasn't disappointed in the panel at all, because I had such low expectations of the con and everything connected to it. The whole clusterfuck of RF09 had made me wary of even attending WisCon 34 due to the utter fails I'd heard of from friends that attended the previous year. I didn't think I could cope with anyone deciding that they had to try and pet the POC, or staring as if they'd never seen one outside of the Eleven O'clock News, or being hauled off in cuffs a la Cops, the TV show that's known for culprits running off into the night—usually shirtless and bewildered as to why the police might be chasing them. I had gotten my fill of RF09 by keeping up with the discussions online and by the conversations being had when I attended WorldCon in July 2009. It seemed that no matter where you went, you could not escape the touch of RF09. It didn't seem as pervasive at WisCon (unless I just missed out on some conversations or somehow tuned it out), except when I was fully present in the moment while discussing RF09 and how it affected the attendees of WisCon 34.

I noticed that the POC safe space was on the main floor, not too far from the hotel lobby, and I wondered why it would be there and not in a more accessible place for con attendees? That was explained via blog posts by con attendees and by people I'd met at WisCon 34: during WisCon 33 the POC safe space was often invaded by folks who either didn't know that set times were exclusively allocated for it, or who just didn't respect the fact that the room was set aside for breathing room for POC con attendees who may have needed a respite from the craziness that is a con, or from a panel full of fail.

Hearing and reading stories like the ones mentioned above made me worry about the whole WisCon experience, but like I've said, the fail I expected did not show itself at all, even at panels where race and othering were the topics of discussion. I think that the negative expectations due to RF09 really pushed me to pick the sessions that I attended in 2010 and in a way made my attendance more about the topic of race, how not to fail, and how to discuss such a volatile topic without it devolving into a flame war or yet more yelling on the internet about how people don't get it, why can't you just stop being so angry, etc. As a POC who often struggles with deciding when to speak up about racial issues and when to stop and consider whether things are actually racist, I found that the experience of WisCon's panels on race, othering, body autonomy, and other issues gave me a good base for discussions that will happen whether I want them to or not.

Now before you get the idea that I only went to the POC-centric panels and didn't really do much besides worry about race and expect fail to jump out of the potted plants at me, I did have a wonderful time at non-race-focused panels and parties. I was even interviewed for the dissertation project of an attendee. This attendee was doing her "overambitious dissertation," which in her own words is "a self-reflexive documentary exploring women and the identity of being a science fiction fan." She wanted to get interviews with sf/f fans of color while at WisCon.

One of the more amusing and lighter moments for me was "Revenge of Not Another F*cking Race Panel." This session did everything but toss the kitchen sink at attendees and panelists in a game show format where participants discussed anything *except* race in an effort to get the point across that we are more than the color of our skin, and our experience as POC is not all that makes us who we are. It was a great break from the serious discussions being had in other rooms, and it was a breath of much needed air after a morning of heavy topics. OK, that was sort-of-kind-of race related, but it was one of the best moments of the con for me, and one panel where I laughed my ass off.

Julia Starkey holds the game wheel for "Revenge of Not Another F*cking Race Panel" and looks down upon the proceedings, while her assistant Sumana Harihareshwara looks up.

Cecilia Tan, Shweta Thakrar, Julia Starkey, Andrea Hairston, and Amal El-Mohtar enjoy a round of "Revenge of Not Another F*cking Race Panel" as Sumana Harihareshwara wields the wheel.

Overall it was the wonderful folks in attendance who made the con for me; they are why I'm already booked for WisCon 35. During the three-and-a-half days of the con, I met folks I'd known only through electronic media. I also made the acquaintance of fine folks who were seasoned con-goers; they put me at ease in an environment that was new, a little scary and had the potential to be utterly full of fail and off-putting. Yes, the sessions are important, but if you wind up in the company of people who make you comfortable and allow you to be you, race, creed, nationality, gender expression, sexual orientation aside, then a convention can be a wonderful experience regardless of panels, parties, and the trip there and back.

My first WisCon met and exceeded my dismal expectations as a fan of color due to the people, late night chats, great food, and wide spectrum of topics covered by the session offerings. In closing, thank you to everyone who made WisCon 34 a great experience for me, kept me from wigging out when there were too many people, and made me realize make-up isn't something to run screaming from as if it may attack me when I'm not looking ;)

Guess Who Came to Dinner

Photographs by Alberto Yáñez
Captions by Nisi Shawl

On Friday, May 28, 2010, K. Tempest Bradford hosted a dinner for WisCon 34's POC in a private room of the Madison Concourse Hotel's restaurant. More than 50 people attended."

K. Tempest Bradford and Minal Hajratwala toast the evening's outstanding attendance.

Julia Starkey and Isabelle Schecter discuss things.

Maurice Broaddus and Moondancer Drake conversate.

Smiling and talking before the food arrives. From left to right: Zola Mumford, LaShawn M. Wanak, Keyan Bowes, Maria Velazquez and Na'amen Tilahun.

Multiple simultaneous discussions featuring expressions of delight, interest, concern, and watchfulness. From left to right: Benazeer Noorani, Candra K. Gill, Maria Velazquez, Sumana Harihareshwara, Nisi Shawl, Tanya C. DePass, and Jessica Kaiser.

At some point, something appalling must have happened to someone somewhere, but Jessica is unfazed. Jessica Kaiser, Jaymee Goh, and Maurice Broaddus.

Stylin with Maria Velazquez and Julia Starkey.

N.K. Jemisin, Mikki Kendall, and Alberto Yáñez smile for Alberto's camera after their meal.

N.K. Jemisin and K. Tempest Bradford settle the bills.

Racial Identity and Writing: A Dozen Writers and Thinkers Reflect — Part One

edited by Eileen Gunn

What does race — your racial identity or that of other people — have to do with what you write?

Andrea Hairston: We have made race a meaningful part of human identity, so it is critical for me to consider that when creating a story world. I trust my intuition. I write to discover. But I am part of a story world with hidden dimensions and secret codes—I must wrestle with the hidden world that made me. It's good for my art.

Claire Light: Uh...this is a huge question and requires a complex answer. But I'll give you a short one instead, in sentence fragments. Mixed race. Apparent on my face. (Hey, that rhymes!) Makes people's heads spin. Since childhood. Lots of questions. Lots of aggression. Lots of ostracism, condescension, silencing, finger-pointing. Outsider crap. Nerd crap. Inferiority complex. Rage. Loss of language. Twist of culture. Geographical displacement. Etc. All very motivating to a writer. Also: endless source of content!

Yoon Ha Lee: I used to write in white futures and white settings, because I was emulating what I saw in the sf/f that I had grown up reading. In the past few years, I have consciously tried to write stories that break away from that, whether they're stories that specifically draw on my Korean heritage or stories that are more generally non-Western in tone. I'm pretty much prepared to do this until someone tells me that there's a glut of Korean-flavored sf/f being published in English.

Nick Mamatas: Race (and racism) is a total surround in this society. Most of my work is set in the modern day or the very near-future, and generally involves characters with no special immunity to racism; a few of my characters are bumbling leftists unfamiliar with how racist their own actions and attitudes often are. So race and identity come up about as often as traffic and the weather and text messaging—very often.

Gavin Grant: I tend to think of race throughout the process, more consciously at some points than others. I'm an immigrant—albeit a white, male, middle-class one—and am very conscious of the differences between natives and incomers. Identity is always in flux, which I find is a major fascination in my writing.

Mark Rich: Being half one thing and half another—Anglo-Swiss and Japanese—I have never quite known what it feels like to know one's racial "identity." Lately it has occurred to me that my writing and musical sides arise more from my Caucasian background, while my graphic-artistic side arises more from my Japanese background—simply on the grounds of who did what, in my respective family-branches.

All the same, I feel contrasting creative impulses that push me in different directions, and these two directions might correspond to the two backgrounds. First, I feel a strong attraction to extreme compression, stylization, and simplification. I would find it hard, though not impossible, to argue against this being Japanese. Second, I am drawn to pursue the expansive forms of fiction and historical narrative. The latter especially requires a wide grasp and a fullness of phrasing, as well as an ability to deal with a considerable amount of surface detail. The conflict between these tendencies—believe me—has caused me no end of difficulties, and has, I believe, slowed my development as a writer, even though I can be an extremely fast writer.

My first tendency sometimes pushes me off in a sound direction, only to leave me with too little on the page; so to fix that, I will at times toe the cliff-edge of overcompensation to the point of toppling over, with my typewriter plunging alongside, into the abyss of overwriting. (I have not found Japanese writers there in that abyss. I am not saying they are not there. I just have not found them.) Many, if not all, of my stories contain within them something of this conflict—perhaps as a problem, perhaps as an invisible tension. Whether it is akin to the pronounced, self-conscious tension in Picasso's etchings, between the Goya and Rembrandt impulses, I am not quite sure. I would like to think not.

That I cannot seem to write the sort of stories, or even the sort of sentences, that most other people write seems clear to me, however.

Doselle Young: On the surface, I'd have to say that my racial identity and that of other people have very little or nothing to do with what I write. Indeed, there's a part of me that simply doesn't care, that's happy to offer quite a bit of push-back for even being presented with the question. After all, it's unlikely the same question will come up the next time someone interviews Stephen King. And therein rests one of the most difficult things that come to mind around the topic of race: the idea that neither I nor other people of color get absolute control over how my or their identity is perceived, even amongst *other* people of color.

Not that I take this personally, mind you. It's simply an observation. And if my ethnic origins have a demonstrable influence on what I write, I would say it gives me an awareness that one's racial identity is part and parcel of a larger stochastic process; important, but only one membrane of the multi-layered interface that exists somewhere between the internal and exterior world.

Ben Rosenbaum: A good and troubling question.

There are two kind of superimposed narratives here.

Race is something that makes sense only in the context of racism; it proceeds from racism. No racism, no race. We live in a historical moment—the moment since about 1560 or so—in which racism is an enormously powerful and potent force, part of the organizing order of the world, the world system. It's not a monolithic or total system, and there has been, over the last 200 years or so, an accelerating series of victories against it—even as that system has responded by becoming more complex and subtle. So here in 2011, we get Obama as Commander-in-Chief of the world's empire, but at the same time, the general questions of "O, inhabitant of earth chosen at random, do you have enough to eat? Where are you safe? What does the world seem to think you should be doing?" still cannot be usefully answered without reference to race; and despite some fragile pockets of privilege in which race is allowed to matter less, race alone provides, statistically, depressingly predictable answers to them in general.

That phenomenon, though, race—as a construct invented during, and for, the age of European colonization—is a recent historical innovation. It's one specific way of globally ordering local xenophobias. Race is new-ish, but xenophobias are as old as large groups of primates at least. Before Europe invented race-as-we-know-it as a meta-order for xenophobias, it had a different ordering mechanism called Christendom. When Joshua slaughtered the inhabitants of Canaan, that genocide was not racial in the modern sense. Intertribal genocide only becomes racial genocide once you have a pseudoscientific system in place to extend its logic across many continents.

Well, enough theory.

For me personally, as a human being?

I am white; I grew up white, in Northern Virginia. In Virginia, race is very clear and brutally defined, and comes down to the question (and the knowledge, constant and intuitive, though never stated aloud) of who would have been the slaves and who the owners. Race herded us into groups already as kids, and in Northern Virginia those groups were pretty much—in terms of the social landscape of the lunchroom—black and maybe Hispanic on one side, and white on the other, with East and South Asians making awkward inroads. I was clearly white; I was in the same group, racially (would have sat at the same lunchtable with) Kirk and Spock and Luke and Han. Cops were polite to me, when I put on my good-boy (oh-gee-I-had-no-idea-how-fast-I-was-going) manners, and perhaps more to the point I could put them on without any uncomfortable sense that I was selling myself out, or in peril; rather, I was just being polite. Teachers expected me to be smart.

If anything that I was Jewish was, in the context of school and the playground, a way of being particularly white; it meant, after all, that teachers expected me to be even smarter, and that I was assumed to possess even less of anything compensatory in the way of rhythm, style, or "street smarts."

I was not only white, but male and unimpeachably upper-middle class (actually, just the perfect class, for the American narrative—rich enough to have a big house, a weekly maid, and Caribbean vacations, but not so rich as to be in danger of inheriting enough wealth to make me indolent, and thus subject to pity and mockery). It was understood that I was headed for the Ivy League. It was understood that the government and the police and the banks and the teachers and the insurance companies were there to protect and provide for me, and smooth my path, and shepherd me to whatever greatness I was destined for—that things would be handled for me, that the world's Empire would put all its efforts into making sure my world was as safe and perfect as possible, whatever happened elsewhere. I have been swimming in white privilege since I was conceived.

At the same time, it was rarely far from my thoughts that, thirty years before and an eight-hour plane ride away, my third and fourth and fifth cousins had been enslaved and shot and starved and gassed and burned for being considered, in that not at all distant place and time (my father's childhood, my grandmother's pen pals), the wrong race. Which made race seem a more fragile and random and imaginary and dangerous matter for me, perhaps, than it did for the other white kids.

And certainly there was a whole other rubric, a much older and broader historical narrative—the one rehearsed every year at Passover—in which being Jewish was a central category, and one connoting risk and danger.

That I was dark—enough so to be regularly mistaken for South Asian—also seemed irrelevant to me, an amusing coincidence that a few moment's conversation could clear up; though, on some level, it might have added to the unease. It's only as an adult that it's begun to seem perhaps more significant: since moving to Switzerland, where I'm not quite so white, and particularly since last WisCon, when I did a little informal survey and discovered to my amazement that the majority of the people of color I surveyed thought—in some cases insisted—that I wasn't white at all....

For me as a writer?

Such questions—the mapping of memory to imagination, of biography to fiction—are always difficult and fraught. But I think that dual consciousness—of being the inheritor of massive privilege and also of outsider risk—is never that far away.

The Russ Categories

by MJ Hardman

Introduction

Hombres necios que acusáis
a la mujer sin razón,
sin ver que sois la occasion
de lo mismo que culpáis:[1]

This I read, once upon a time, when I was learning Spanish: the work of Sor Juana Inés de la Cruz,[2] a 17th century Mexican nun, giving me the first insight into the way we talk being closely tied to the way we treat people and conceive of people, and of the great hypocrisy of the station of women. The word "sexism" had not yet been invented, so I couldn't say it was that. She became a hero of mine and way back then I could recite all the verses, but memory now only gives me the first.

At the time I had never heard of science fiction. Instead, in Perú as a Fulbright student, I met a very interesting man who for some twenty years had been looking for a linguist to help him learn to read and write his own language, given that the Spanish alphabet was obviously inadequate. At the time he needed to learn English for a grant he had for traveling to the United States, so we sat across the table and taught each other our languages. Here was the next great discovery: in Jaqaru the sexes are not ranked. By then the word "sexism" had been invented and I could say: Jaqaru was *not* sexist—nor was the culture. For the first time in my life I was treated as a full human. I developed the theoretical construct of the Linguistic Postulate,[3] first introduced in Spanish[4] and then in English in a memorial volume for my mentor.[5] I had to develop this theory in order to have a way to discuss this amazing discovery (a discovery only on my part—the Tupe people had known it all along) with those who didn't know about it. Curiously, at the time the theory was roundly rejected—not part of the canon and not believable. But I have lived it these 50 years now.

Then, at a particular time when I received some nasty blows of sexism—of the "we shall overwork you, underpay you, and then blame you when others misbehave"[6] variety—I found myself compelled to understand why those who claimed to be nonsexist and nonracist had acted so badly, and why the only support I received came from an untenured black woman professor who, in the end, left the University of Florida because of this. So I applied my Linguistic Postulate theory to my own language. What I found has turned out to be far more productive than I would have imagined it to be in those early years, though it did describe the thinking of those who treated me so badly.[7]

Derivational Thinking

The three postulates of English that helped this attack happen and that have turned up everywhere in more ways that I could ever have imagined are number (singular/plural), hierarchy (-er, -est, more, less and the lexicalized versions, best, worst, better, etc.), and sex-based gendered hierarchy (starting with pronouns, vocabulary, and the "generic" masculine). These feed on one another, each strengthening the other.

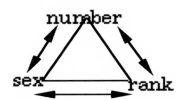

The theoretical construct of derivational thinking explains how our grammar sabotages our ideologies of equality of being and opportunity; it shows us how we create and recreate hierarchies, making differences become deficiencies, and separating groups of people in ways that have many negative consequences.[8]

Some works of science fiction show that we can transcend our grammar, that we can take advantage of the flexibility that is there in all languages. Ursula K. Le Guin does this in *Always Coming Home*. She translates from a language that is yet to exist. The really fun part comes when students who are SF fans believe her because it is so difficult to read until you get used to it.

In this essay I am looking at the all day everyday speech that keeps the structure of the status quo going in spite of our ideology: not the big things, but the little things that are the foundations of the big ones.

Cheswam

There came the problem that every time I tried to explain the structure of the status quo and used the phrase "white man," every young man in the class would react negatively. No explanation that I was talking about *structure*, not individuals ever went anywhere. So I invented a new word. And it does work. It allows a perfectly grammatical and intelligible sentence like, "The former Secretary of State has *cheswam* values." Furthermore, we can discuss the issues and no one becomes uncomfortable.

Patriarchal cultures privilege male and male-identified groups/things/values. In the US, privilege accrues to the culturally hierarchical, English-speaking, white, American, male and male-identified—that is, to the cheswam (pronounced chee-swahm: "che" as in cheese; "swahm" as in swami). Many people of all sexes and races hold cheswam values; if they did not, all that we are talking about here would not work. Learning cheswam values is a matter of the acquisition of language/culture, usually occurring by the age of six, not unchangeable, but not easily changed, either.

SF

About this time I did discover SF, thanks to the Quechua spoken in a bar scene in the film *Star Wars* (a curious story itself). Among the authors I first read was Joanna Russ, and very shortly her nonfiction work *How to Suppress Women's Writing*.[9] There, on page 18, I found what I had not known I had been looking for:

> To act in a way that is both sexist and racist, to maintain one's class privilege, it is only necessary to act in the customary, ordinary, usual, even polite manner.

As they say, nothing was quite the same ever again.

I loved Joanna's Glottlogs[10] and attempted to incorporate them in my work; I called the examples I created in emulation of hers *glottologalisms*. I still would, but for those for whom sf is alien the term never worked. I would love to receive some glottologalisms from WisCon folk.

The Russ Categories

Joanna's book consists of nine chapters, each describing a way to suppress women's writing, plus some material not of interest here. From the beginning I saw in these categories an opportunity to guide the perceptions of students within my theoretical construct of derivational thinking, to give them further categories to learn to hear and to observe, and to apply them to people of color (POC), the disabled, and other marginalized groups.[11] As a teaching tool, the Russ Categories have succeeded beyond my wildest expectations.

Anita Taylor and I have worked and reworked Joanna's categories. However much they now differ from her originals and no matter what we say[12] it needs to be known that she and I stand on the shoulders of Joanna Russ. Thank you, Joanna, for opening this door for me that I was then able to open for Anita and then for so many, many more. That we stand on your shoulders must never be ignored nor forgotten.

All of the Russ Categories are about good, creative, appropriate accomplishments. Joanna worked with writing; we include everything in the universe, providing the agent is a woman or a person of color and that what is done is worthwhile in some way. The subject of a sentence is the actor. This is distinguished from being an object, which is acted upon. *To have agency is to have subject status.*

All of the Russ Categories can be used viciously, of course, in witch-hunts, against individuals of any kind (take a look at politics). That is not what we are looking at here. Remember the quote above from Joanna's book. We are looking at *cultural discourse patterns* that we use all day, every day, usually utterly obliviously. In English we rank object and subject, with the subject *always* ranked higher than the object. In linguistics we speak of "raising the object to subject position." Knowing the derivational thinking templates of English we can easily understand that the higher ranked *subject* is preferably singular and also white male; object(s) may be those who aren't "real" people, like women and people of color (POC). Therefore, the most comfortable grammatical sentence in English, if it is a sentence of accomplishment, is one that has a singular (white) male as the subject. However, other people do do things. And that must be coped with. That's done with a series of discourse patterns first identified by Joanna Russ in *How to Suppress Women's Writing*, which is why the discovery of her book was so exciting to me. I had only recently invented the Derivational Thinking Theoretical Construct—and here was something from SF that fit right in.

Remember, we are talking here about *subjects* who *accomplish* something. The patterns show how, when women or POC achieve and the achievement can't be dismissed, it will be treated as a negative accomplishment in some way.

In each case there is a brief introduction identifying the pattern, followed by an identifier or *Definer,* which is a case that defines the patterns. Following the Definer, there are some examples supplied by my students over the past years up to and including spring of 2010. One amazing/shocking observation on my part is that the ease of finding examples (and it is amazingly easy) has not changed over the years. Culture trumps ideology.

Sometimes I include comments.

Two Categories of Less Concern to Us

The first Russ Category (Prohibitions), even when I began teaching on this subject, was mostly gone in terms of outright, absolute prohibitions. This topic, after one attempt otherwise, I always covered in lecture form. Long gone already were the '60s and '70s directives and laws such as "Women can't buy houses," "Women can't borrow money from banks," "Women can't have pension benefits," "Women's families are not entitled to Social Security if they die," "Women can't cash checks (Dr. Hardman *himself* is not here)," "Women can't have credit cards"—some of you remember the rest; though for some of you this will be news.

In my own case, because I am a woman I could not declare my foreign husband as a relative for visa privileges. That right was reserved for men, who *could* declare their foreign wives as relatives and receive visas to bring them into the US.[13]

Even longer gone—for many locales—were the Prohibitions of the '40s and '50s: "Women (and girls) can't wear trousers," "Women (and girls) can't ride boys' bikes," "Women (and girls) can't play marbles" "Women (and girls) can't enroll in math classes," "Women (and girls) can't enroll in shop." One of the reasons I have not retired is that I think the young'uns need to know where they came from and what we did for them, lest they lose it again. Mostly they don't quite believe it. They better, or history may repeat itself.

Joanna's second category, Bad Faith, is more than obvious to participants, but requires too much circumstantial knowledge to work in a live presentation. A good read, however.

(Plain) Denial of Agency

The third of the Russ Categories, Denial of Agency, is the first we'll focus on:[14] "If the accomplishment is something good, she did it, but she didn't, some man did." This becomes "POC did it, but POC didn't do it, some white dude did." Or some *thing* did. Denial of Agency finds some other agent to replace the unwanted agent in the subject slot. Here are two additional definitions of Denial of Agency, contributed by students:

> If a person who has achieved something magnificent is a woman, or of an ethnic background that is not White, the white men in power would try to deny that achievement or the person: Nothing has been done, and no one did it. Denial of Agency is considered as a means for the few white men to secure their "sole" superior status. [You can find the three English postulates of sex-based gender, comparative ranking, and number, in this example.] [Courtesy Chun Huang]

> Denial of agency is an act on the part of one person that ignores another's contributions. The denial may be conscious or subconscious, but the happening is used consistently in society to maintain an imbalance of power and achievement between the dominant members and the minorities. [Courtesy Kerry Linfoot-Ham]

The Definer example:

> I was sitting in the waiting room, playing with Jamie. One of her favorite games is to grab my fingers for stability, and muscle her way up into a stand. A woman saw us playing this game, and came over and said, "What a strong little boy you are, able to stand up on your own like that!" I answered, "She is very strong, isn't she?" The woman looked surprised, and commented, "She's so big for a little girl. And you're so cute, and letting daddy pull you up like that." [Courtesy Art Bautista-Hardman]

The baby, if a boy, pulls himself up; if a girl, is pulled up by Daddy. Agency is attributed to the handiest male. This is a Definer because it is coming entirely from cultural perceptions, out of courtesy in a boring waiting room. There is no agenda and everyone is behaving politely.

Sometimes the "man" is at a remove:

> I had one glaring example of a denial of agency at my church last Sunday. A male visitor (who appeared to be around "senior citizen" age) commented on what a good organist we have. "The organist certainly plays well, doesn't he?" was his comment to me. When I politely responded that the organist is indeed very good, but corrected him on his assumption that our organist is male, he responded, "Well, I always did like Mozart, anyway." Anyway? Suddenly the organist's talent is unimportant, and the male composer is responsible for the music. [Courtesy Anna Davis]

Sometimes the agency is attributed to an instrument:

> This weekend a bunch of us got together to play softball. I admit my roommate and I, the only women playing, were not hitting the ball very far. Yet when finally I hit a decent ground drive and was safe on first, a friend yelled, "Good hit; which bat was that?" I guess he thought the bat deserved as much credit as I did. [Courtesy Kathy Smith]

Sometimes agency is attributed to "the-man-within-her:"

> My housemate, a single female, is in the process of trying
> to refinance her mortgage. She has done lots of mainte-
> nance and improvements prior to the visit of the apprais-
> er, including using a chainsaw to remove some overgrown
> bushes/trees in front of the house. A neighbor (retired
> male professor) complimented her on the improvements
> telling her, "You're a good man." [Courtesy Ruth Trocolli]

Denial of Agency happens to POC, for example when the then-president
of a certain university publicly called the only black member of the
Board of Trustees "an oreo." Similarly, in the following example:

> A close friend of mine in high school was black. When
> speaking of him to newcomers or just in casual conversa-
> tion people would often say, "Jaie is not really black—he
> is a white guy trapped in a black man's body." [Courtesy
> Elizabeth Williams]

Sometimes the accomplishment itself is denied; that is, what has been
accomplished isn't really an accomplishment, as in this example:

> When I was in 10th grade, I took the PSAT (Preliminary
> Scholastic Aptitude Test) not knowing that in the future
> it could possibly pay for my undergraduate education.
> As I navigated my way through my college search, more
> and more schools began to offer me both partial and full
> scholarships because of my test scores.... After I signed
> my scholarship paperwork and made it through the sum-
> mer PAACT (Pledging to Achieve Academic Competence
> Together) program, school started. Usually the National
> Achievement Scholarship is grouped with the National
> Merit Scholarship, but for some reason a young man I
> encountered thought that he should point out to me that
> I got the "black" people scholarship. At first I thought
> that he was simply referring to the fact that the National
> Achievement scholarship is only for minorities while the
> National Merit Scholarship can be won by anyone, but he
> then proceeded to inform me that the only reason I got

into this university and managed to get them to pay for my education was because I am black and the admissions office needed to boost numbers. According to him, my sole qualification for the scholarship was the color of my skin and not my academic achievements.... Someone once said to me that if I ever make it big I should make sure that I do not tell anyone that I am Jamaican because everyone will know that I had to have bribed someone to get where I was because the only thing Jamaicans know how to do is smoke weed. [Courtesy Serena M. Rose]

Children learn to deny agency to groups of people early. They are taught it as the "correct" way to view the world. It also is appropriate for men to assume credit for any accomplishment of a woman:

One example which stands out in my mind involves a kindergarten experience. I was in kindergarten class, and I sat and watched Nicole build a small cottage out of the blocks we had to play with. I soon joined her and we sat and played. The teacher came by and admired the work and congratulated me on this work of art. I smiled and pointed in Nicole's direction and the teacher looked at her and said, "Oh, she helped too, isn't that sweet." [Courtesy Christopher Morrison]

Last week Leah, my coworker, made a paper airplane for a five-year-old named Kyle. After she handed him the plane, he went running around the playground yelling, "Hey, everybody, look what I made." Eventually, the plane fell out of shape and he came to me to fix it. I told him that if he actually made the plane in the first place, he should have no trouble repairing it. He insisted that he was the creator of the plane, so I continued to refuse help. Finally, after Kyle made enough fuss that there were several of his peers around him, he admitted that Leah made the plane for him. I then repaired it. [Courtesy Tamara Sniad]

The second example shows how we can begin to change the cultural patterns, one drop at a time.

We even learn to deny our own agency if we are POC, women, or otherwise identified as marginal:

> Last semester, my roommate, Wendy, and I got locked out of our apartment. The males from across the street came over with a butter knife to help us pick the lock. I could see that their approach was all wrong, but, for some unknown reason, I stood there watching quietly. As soon as they gave up, I offered my services. (My roommate laughed saying that she would definitely want to witness it.) I got the door open and the two of us thanked the males profusely for all of their help. [Courtesy Tamara Sniad]

Pollution of Agency

If there is absolutely no way that one can deny that a woman or a POC has actually accomplished something, then one way of making sure that it doesn't count is to assault her character. If she is of bad character, then one does not have to actually credit the accomplishment and she is effectively removed from the subject slot. Pollution of Agency consists of imputing unpleasant traits to agents to deflect recognition of their agency.

Because our society invests so much of its moral judgment in sex, sex is the major way of polluting the agency of someone one wishes to remove from the subject slot. In fact, sex is used so very often to pollute agency that we divide the pollution into types. Other categories of pollution include crazy, criminal, and defective (there are several types of defective). These pollutions are irrelevant to the actual accomplishment and frequently false; in fact, they are often proffered simply upon learning of the sex or race of the accomplisher, with no sense that they should be investigated. But even if they were true, or even partially true, they would be irrelevant to the accomplishment and would be so perceived if the accomplisher were a white man.

The Definer below shows three categories: pollution by sex of the type "not enough sex," by crazy, and by defective, in this case by defective appearance. And all in one sentence! This is a Definer example because there is no agenda, only cultural/linguistic perceptions. The people do not know each other; the judgment is made exclusively on the basis of the sex of accomplisher:

> A male friend of mine has a video game for his computer called "Duke Nukem 3D." The game includes a program that allows people to create their own maps. Making a map is a long, arduous task that requires hours, even days of work. Many people make their maps available on the internet so that other Duke Nukem players can use them. Recently, I was watching my friend play Duke Nukem using a map he had acquired via the internet, when suddenly he exclaimed, "He must not have put any secret doors in this one." Curious, I asked, "How do you know this map was made by a he?" My friend responded, "Of course it was a he! I have yet to see a Duke Nukem map that wasn't made by a he! There are no girls who make these things!" I quickly pointed out to my friend that the past two times we played this game we used a map entitled "Jen's Apartment." The file, I reminded him, had come attached with a note from Jen herself expressing her hopes that players would find her map enjoyable. My friend then replied with something like, "Oh yeah. Well, she's probably some weirdo computer freak with dark circles under her eyes who never leaves the house." [Courtesy Elaine Cantor]

A major category of pollution by sex is to say that she got credit via sex rather than by doing it herself.

> I was talking to a friend about a speech class that I signed up for. When I told him which professor I had, he told me that the professor was extremely difficult and the class was going to be really hard to pass. My first day of class, I realized my friend was right. The professor told us he had high expectations and few, if any of us, would earn As. It became a challenge for me. I did every single assignment, all the readings, and I practiced my speeches to my roommate, my boyfriend, anyone I could force to listen. Finally,

at the end of the semester I nervously got online to check the posted grades. I got an A in the class! I was so thrilled that my hours of hard work and effort had paid off. The next time I saw my friend I told him the good news. He looked at me in disbelief. "Well," he said, "I bet he only gave you an A because you're a cute blonde." [Courtesy Rachelle Detky]

Another common type of pollution by sex is "wrong sex." The "wrong sex" usually used is lesbian or gay. And that, in and of itself, is an issue, as to why that should be so "wrong." Using these patterns helps to solidify and perpetuate bias.

This example is also a Definer—no agenda and no personal knowledge of the person being polluted.

When a friend of mine had finished reading one of the several Star Trek novels written by Vonda N. McIntyre, he appeared truly satisfied with the contents of the book. "I'm impressed," my friend said. "This book wasn't as bad as some of the others. It's probably because that Vonda chick is some strange lesbian who stays locked up in her house all the time except when she dresses up as Mr. Spock to pick up other women." Although he had read many other lacking novels in the same genre (written mostly by men) he never made a comment more than, "That was terrible," or "That sucked." However, when it was actually a good book written by a woman, he had to make a derogatory comment to justify the occurrence. [Courtesy Scott LaPorta]

Another way to pollute through sex is condemn the work because the accomplisher has too *little* sex. Rosalind Franklin did the fundamental work that made possible our current understanding of RNA and DNA. There is a movie that details the denial and pollution of her agency, even to how Crick and Watson broke into her lab to steal her work in order to be able to do theirs. This also includes pollution type "defective" in this case the defectiveness of Franklin's appearance. And when referring to the quotation included below, one might want to ask *whose* emotions were under questionable control.

One of the scientists appearing in *The Double Helix* by James Watson was Rosalind Franklin. According to Watson, however, she was nothing but a nuisance. One part of the book describes how much trouble "Rosy [sic]" was causing because she "would not think of herself as Maurice's assistant:" "I suspect that in the beginning Maurice hoped that Rosy would calm down. Yet mere inspection suggested that she would not easily bend. By choice she did not emphasize her "feminine" qualities. Though her features were strong, she was not unattractive and might have been quite stunning had she taken even a mild interest in clothes. This she did not. There was never lipstick to contrast with her straight black hair, while at the age of 31 her dresses showed all the imagination of English bluestocking adolescents.... There was no denying she had a good brain. If she could only keep her emotions under control there would be a good chance that she could really help him." Because Rosalind did not conform to Watson's standards of "femininity," she was not worthy of respect. Later, while Franklin is giving a presentation on x-ray crystallography, Watson "wondered how she would look if she took off her glasses and did something novel with her hair." Watson judges Franklin as a woman, not as a scientist, and this is a pollution of agency. [and by imputed lack of emotional control—when it was really full control!] [Courtesy Michael Wasson]

One of the categories of pollution by sex is "feminist," which like the "wrong sex" one above is part of the way in which prejudices and discriminations are solidified and perpetuated.

I belong to a book club that meets every month for discussion. Our most recent book had a passage in which the main character (a black man) became enraged at people first-naming him while not first-naming white men in similar positions. One of the members cited this passage as something he (as a white man) could not relate to. I mentioned that women are first-named more than men, and for that reason, maybe the women could relate somewhat better. Later in the discussion, a different member first-named a female author and in the next breath referred to a male author using his last name. "See?" I said. "Don't mind her," said another member, referring to me. "She's taking another one of those weird feminist language classes." [Courtesy Sarah Wears]

Pollution of Agency occurs all day, every day, to great detriment in the effort to construct a society of equality. In the following example John Sheehy shows how easy it was to accomplish his weekly observation assignment:

During the last week I encountered as least five examples of Pollution of Agency: first, after I returned from my haircut appointment, my friend told me, "The guy did a nice job." When I informed him that it was a girl, he responded, "She must have been a lesbian or a real tomboy." Second, while sitting in chemistry class, I heard the guy behind me say to the girl next to him "Who did you f--- to get that grade? That was a damn hard quiz!" When she responded, "No one! I did it all by myself," the student then said "You just flirted with the TA then, huh?" Third, while I was doing my daily workout, I overheard two people talking. There was a girl there doing the leg press with a significant amount of weight about whom the two people were commenting. One said to the other, "What a dyke! She looks like a guy." The other then responded, "I bet she wishes she had a penis." Fourth, at a party one night, several people were standing around discussing President Clinton's impending health-care proposal. While discussing the merits of having Hilary Clinton chair the fact-finding committee, one person stated, "It's very simple; if you have sex with someone every night, then you're bound to have some influence over them, whether you're qualified or not. She's [Hilary] not." Fifth, while my friend and I were walking through the store, a girl walked by who looked like she was a semi-dedicated bodybuilder. My friend commented,

"Geez, she looks like a freak! Why would a girl want to do that to her body? Any girl that does that has some serious psychological problems." [Courtesy John Sheehy]

False Categorization

Joanna's fifth and sixth categories are The Double Standard of Content and False Categorizing. There were several problems with these categories. Joanna herself did not separate the two clearly. I restated them, but year after year the students were confused. When Anita Taylor and I began giving workshops at national conferences we learned that professors had the same problem; "double standard" already has a meaning, and it is not Joanna's. Anita finally suggested that we merge the two; after all, the fifth is also a type of false categorization.

Therefore, our third pattern is, quite simply, False Categorization.

If assaults on the character of the accomplisher don't work to deny the agency, we can always miscategorize the work. Similar to misfiling a paper or a book in the library, miscategorization can cause the accomplishment to disappear.

Miscategorization can be in reference to the substance of the work itself (women and POC are simply not interesting and therefore nothing referring to their lives can be), or it can be to where the work is placed in reference to the rest of all accomplishments (Black studies, Women's studies). Subcategories include: misshelving; not real (domain); experience of no value; not a real person; creator of no value.

One student, Chun Huang, described it thus: "If a man wrote a love story during the wartime, he wrote a 'war' story; if a woman wrote a love story during the wartime, she wrote a 'love' story. And only the war story is considered a masterpiece, but the love story is 'just a love story.' This shows that in the male dominant society, people categorize things more by gender (and race) than just by looking at the content. Even worse, because only men's experience is regarded highly, the works dealing with female experience are often neglected as unimportant or even 'unintelligible' or 'not interesting.' This false categorization applies to race and other social domains as well: rap music is not 'real' music nor is it 'real' poetry, and graffiti is just a 'subcultural' form of art. Moreover, a rapper is not a musician but a 'black' musician, and one who studies women's life is not doing sociology but 'Women's Studies.'"

Definer example—here the experience of the young woman is of no value, not being one in which men participate. (If you don't know what "menarche" means, look it up in a dictionary; then wonder why you didn't know what it meant, and what that has to do with this category.)

> A friend of mine, Mary, is currently taking a creative writing course under a male professor. Last week, when she submitted her first piece she was appalled by the low grade. When she inquired about this matter (after all, she had put her "soul" into this piece as she had told me earlier), he told her that the assignment had been to write about something that changed your life, not menarche! [Courtesy Jeanne M. Sevelius]

Another Definer—here a category is considered "closed" and the creator is of no value; an alternative category for the accomplishment allows the pretense that it does not (really) exist.

> The Cherokee have a person of power in the tribe who fits the white definition of a Medicine Man, but this person is a woman. White Men had trouble dealing with this so they decided that she was really the assistant of the real Medicine Man and called her a "corn woman." [Courtesy Lisa R. Perry]

Misshelving is a major subcategory of False Categorization. Often it happens very close to home:

> My mother is an accomplished triathlete. She has qualified for and completed the Ironman (sic—Ironperson) triathlon in Hawaii, a race comprised of a 2.4 mile swim, a 112 mile bike, and a 26 mile run. She has…a desire to become a sports therapist…. Her interest in the total lifestyle she has been developing is serious…as she continues to accomplish the things required both physically and professionally of her. As her son, I am guilty of falsely categorizing my mother. To me, her accomplishments, despite

the incredible effort involved, always seemed a bit crazy and nothing more than an out of control hobby. Often, I am not interested in the details of her training and racing, and I exercise a large degree of control over the topics chosen and pursued in our conversations.... Because of my false categorization of her achievements and pursuits as not serious or important ("She is not really she [an athlete] and it is not really it [serious, important]"), I deny her the opportunity to participate fully in a conversation as herself, a serious and accomplished athlete. [Courtesy John Thompson]

A major way of falsely categorizing through misshelving is to judge the experience to be of no value:

I took an American Literature course with a focus on disabilities. In one class period we discussed people with physical disabilities and the obstacles they faced in day-to-day exercises. When I joined in the discussion, the teacher asked me how I felt being a black woman (he considered this to be two disabilities); I was puzzled and appalled. After [categorizing me] as disabled, he brought up the book *The Bluest Eye* by Toni Morrison and stated that she was the first black woman (disabled and all) to win the Nobel Prize for Literature. That she is considered a great writer was completely irrelevant to him. [Courtesy Heather Price]

Sometimes the False Categorization is that of devaluing a whole domain as being a "useless" domain and therefore of no interest:

A few weeks ago I heard about a double standard of content that was directed towards a friend of mine. My friend, Tyler, is a student at Santa Fe Community College. She is taking an introductory level course in fashion design and marketing. As a class assignment, the students were asked to write a paper on the specific area of fashion that was of the most interest to them. Tyler, an accomplished seamstress, wrote about the actual production of clothing (cutting patterns, sewing hemlines, etc.). When the papers were returned the students were asked to share what they wrote with the rest of the class. A male stood up and said that he had written about the business/marketing aspect of fashion. He was interested in opening a clothing store that could lead to an eventual chain of stores with a mass-produced catalog. The professor applauded his motivation and excellent business sense. When Tyler shared her paper and talked about how much she loved actually making clothes, the professor almost scoffed. He said that sewing was a fun "hobby" but was at the absolute bottom of the "fashion pyramid" and relatively unimportant.... [Courtesy Rachael Weiss]

Or the domain in which one is working is deemed to be not the "real" domain:

A professor commented it made more sense for "academics" to write books concerning minority and "third" world problems because they would reach a broader audience (and more importantly the "right" audience) than if those same books were written by minorities and residents of third world countries. When I asked why, he said the latter books would only appeal to specialized groups as Black Studies, Women's Studies, etc. [Courtesy Lisa R. Perry]

The dangerous and oppressive aspect of false categorizations—their function—is that potentially great or useful or necessary accomplishments are marginalized and their promise hampered. The marginalized contributions will be thought of as less "serious" and simply frivolous, i.e., unsuitable as subjects for true scholarly investigation, or for ordinary human appreciation, or of any "real" value whatsoever, however necessary they may be to continued existence or reasonable comfort.

Isolation

Joanna's seventh category and our fourth is Isolation. If the accomplishment stands, if it can't be denied by claiming someone/thing else did it, if you can't sufficiently besmirch the character of its accomplisher, if you can't make it disappear by misshelving or miscategorizing the content, you can claim it as a non-accomplishment. That is, we needn't take the accomplishment or its creator seriously because it is only, or just…. The operative words for isolation are "only" and "just." The accomplishment is isolated from the whole body of work it relates to and made to stand as though it *were* the whole body of work, then trivialized as "just."

To quote my student Chun Huang: "What happens when a minority person's achievement is not deniable, nor can her personality and work be polluted or falsely categorized? Well, then, this person must be the *only one* of them…that is so great. Or this person has done *only one* great thing that has helped her join the group of the great."

Or to quote my student Kerry Linfoot-Ham: "A dangerous aspect of Isolation is that frequently a woman's or minority's other achievements may be overlooked…. In this way, a single achievement is required to be phenomenal in order for its legacy to continue throughout history. Men and other dominant parties, on the other hand, may accumulate a series of, perhaps lesser, achievements that may add up and eventually allow his fame or infamy to be remembered past his own lifetime. Following this methodology, a female or minority person is, therefore, required to produce a work of genius in order to be recognized—especially if only one aspect of their work is to be taken into consideration in the assessment of their worth."

As Joanna says, "Isolation is the myth of the isolated achievement." Occasionally there is real "beginner's luck," or a genuinely unique creation, but the nature of human abilities is that they come from somewhere and form part of the pattern of personality. But Isolation denies that, so the accomplishment will not be seen as part of the identity of the "wrong" people.

Note that Isolation doesn't yet have a Definer that I am satisfied with—perhaps one of you will provide it! The closest is one that happened to me. A white male professor wrote a book on the history of women at the University of Florida (where I have taught since 1969). He so generously included me, composing one sentence on my contributions. He sent me that sentence, which stated that my work was language and gender. I wrote back saying that yes, indeed, that was true, but really my primary area of specialization was the languages of South America; I had written grammars, etc. So he sent back the revised sentence, and gender was gone entirely. I could be only one thing. This isn't quite a definer, though close, because I cannot be absolutely sure there was not an agenda behind it.

I didn't buy the book.

Isolation can be achieved by designating the accomplishment as beginner's luck:

> At my sister's workplace there is a water jug which must be filled with containers of eight gallons of water. Last week when the dispenser was empty, a female employee asked one of the men to replace the somewhat heavy jug. Since everyone was "busy" my sister, Christine, took the task upon herself. Her passive audience insisted that the endeavor would be unsuccessful: "You're gonna spill it!" Christine carried the jug to the dispenser and quickly flipped it without spilling a drop, to which one member of her audience responded... "Yeah, you didn't spill any this time but you'll never do that again." [Courtesy Annice Bouani]

Isolation can be also achieved by burying any notice of other work done:

> Bob Marley, the Jamaican reggae icon, was accompanied on most of his best recordings by a female trio, the I-Threes. Individually, these women had successful careers of their own. This is attested by their numerous awards and international recognition. Unfortunately, those achievements were never singled out on their merits. These solo artists were generally identified [as] Bob Marley's harmonizers. As for their personal achievements, they have become irrelevant and inconsequential. [Courtesy Glen Owen]

A common way of achieving isolation is by picking one work as the whole:

> When my husband and I got our first computer, we had it delivered to his parents' house, where his brother was also staying. I indicated that I would put the system together and configure it, and both my father- and brother-in-law insisted that they would do it. I told them that I had extensive experience with computer systems and they replied, "But you have only worked with one kind of system—Unix—and this one is different." They knew I was very experienced with computers, but they isolated my achievement to one type of system and ignored my other experience. [Courtesy Kathy Phillips]

In the above case, endless application of Russ Categories (which she by then could name and thus begin to cope with) eventually persuaded this student *not* to continue to the PhD in science.

Sometimes isolation is achieved by ranking a whole domain as "only" or "just:"

> Today the Honors Forum was addressed by President Arias, former president of Costa Rica and winner of the 1987 Nobel Peace Prize. As I was sitting waiting for the presentation to begin, I overheard a conversation going on behind me. A woman was commenting to her friend that this forum should be interesting since we were to be addressed by a Nobel Peace Prize winner. Her friend immediately denied that statement by saying "He only worked in Central America; I don't know why he won an award." This statement struck me as isolation because the man's statement implied that Central America is an unimportant part of the world and so any work done there is limited in its affect on topics of real importance, say the affairs of white men. I can safely say that peace brought to the countries of Central America by President Arias is of great importance to the millions of people living there. [Courtesy Kelley Galvin]

Anomalousness

When all the other ways of denying agency have been tried, and found wanting, one can always fall back on "weird." And whoever is "weird" does not need to be taken into account, so the canon holds.

The following example is a superb Definer:

> Driving around this afternoon, I saw a sign that read "Men at Work" on the side of the road and I commented to my girlfriend that this sign might be the last sign to ever have to be changed to "People at Work," because I had never seen a woman working on road repairs and therefore the sign still holds true.... However, she quickly called my attention to a woman we had both seen and commented on the day before, who was working on drainage pipes by the roadside. Oddly enough, she quickly dismissed her own example as invalid because she was "weird." Indeed we had both perceived this woman to be weird the day before, this being why we had commented on and remembered her. She was an odd-looking woman with an extremely heavy build and dressed in a stereotypically male uniform. Regardless of her appearance, which in truth is irrelevant, my girlfriend had cited her as an example in our little joke and then quickly disregarded her, because she did not fit the mold. [Courtesy Carlos Martinez]

These patterns are, in order to work, fully internalized:

> At a recent gathering, a friend remarked that he didn't want to do anything he would regret later. Despite the fact that both my roommate and I were present and female, I replied that he needn't worry, there weren't any girls around. To his, "Oh...no girls, huh?" I said, "Yes, we [my roommate and I] don't count!" I dismissed my roommate and myself as anomalies in the all-male room. [Courtesy Shannon]

Anomalousness is a way of dismissing, of making nonexistent, a way of not counting, and it can be applied to oneself. These patterns continue to work until one recognizes them, names them, and decides not to use them. These are not trivial matters. They can impact our very sense of identity and can have important consequences for life decisions:

> All my life I feel I have been a victim of anomalousness. I have always been very active in sports, and because of this both females and males have made me feel strange, different, an anomaly. When I was in elementary school I enjoyed exploring the woods and playing in creeks. I remember two incidents involving my friends' parents that are an example of anomalousness. One day when I called a female friend to come over and play, she told me her mother wanted to talk to my mother. I listened on the other line, and I could not believe it when my friend's mother informed my mom that her daughter could not play with me anymore. She said I was too rough and tomboyish, and she didn't feel this was appropriate for her daughter, who she wanted to grow up a lady. Another time when I was over at a male friend's house and we asked his father if we could go out and play. His father looked at me and said, "What are you going to do, play house?" He then proceeded to kid his son about playing with a girl, and asked him, "You want to grow up to be a man, don't you? Find some boys to play with. I don't think Karen's parents would like her playing with the boys all the time anyway. Don't you have any girl friends?" he asked me. Both of these incidents made me feel weird and out of place when I was a child. Actually, I still feel odd, and I think things like this that happened throughout my childhood have affected me more deeply than I realized. Anomalousness isolates the victim from both females and males. In these two incidents I was told I was too rough an influence on girls, yet if I played with the boys I might turn them into sissies. I feel anomalousness is one of the most deeply scarring incidents out of Joanna Russ's observations, especially on a child. [Courtesy Karen Motz]

This category, and the others, can keep us from perceiving people who would be compatible with us, people with whom we could form community. They do, indeed, keep community from being anything but that admitted by canon.

This case was addressed to the instructor:

I must admit my own bias. When I first heard your lectures on race and gender, I thought you were a mad, angry white woman. I thought your derivational thinking theory was a big joke. I was wrong for thinking like that. But please understand my prejudice. In my whole entire life, I have never seen or heard any white person, including white women, talking with such a passion and authority on behalf of the less fortunate like you do. So, to me, it was weird to hear a white woman talking about equality, justice, and respect for all cultures. But as I got to know you better, and as you started to open my eyes, I came to learn to admire you for your honesty and passion. My prejudice is a good example of what Joanna Russ refers to as anomalousness. Because you are isolated from liberated writers like your own self, you appeared bizarre to me. In my eyes, you were unique. I did not know there are thousands of writers like you out there. As a result, I did not see your work as a serious and objective work. But what is objectivity anyway? Now, thanks to you, I know it is just a way to keep compassionate feminist writers and thinkers like you from writing. Thanks to you I [am] free from derivational thinking and [can] overcome my own prejudice. [Courtesy Jeff Moussignac]

Lack of Models

Joanna's ninth and last category, and for us the sixth, is lack of models—we have no one to emulate. In the early years of teaching this class, this was a major item. I found a book on women with patents and sent students to the library where I'd reserved it to find a hero they would have liked to have known about when they were young; I asked them to write a page or two on the subject to give to a young student. Then came the book of women philosophers, and then the one on women explorers, and now there's an avalanche, including numerous websites. Models pop up all the time on Book TV even. So lack of models is no longer the problem for women that it once was. When I teach, nevertheless, the assignment persists.[15] Because these categories can be applied to other marginalized groups, there continues to be a lack of models for those belonging to them, in many, many arenas.

Passive Exonerative

We have discussed the Russ Categories, which are all about how to keep women *out* of the subject slot. There is one case where, as English is spoken in the here and now, women are preferred in the subject slot: if they are victims. This neatly hides the perp (frequently a white male) and makes her problems look like her agency. The grammatical structure most often used for this is the passive voice:

"The woman was raped at the frat house."

or

"The woman got raped at the frat house."

Compare these to:

"The frat boys raped the woman."

Then go watch the news, read the headlines. This is the reverse of the Russ Categories; it protects those who should be taking responsibility.

Order

In English order matters. That which comes first is considered "better" in some way. Also in English, feminine forms are derived from masculine (Paulette < Paula; actress < actor, etc.). "Woman" and "female" are not derived etymologically from "man" and "male," but folk etymology so has it, which is part of the rationale for believing in feminine derivation. Therefore, the result is that if the feminine is placed second it is heard as the derivation of the first, if heard at all. On the other hand, if the feminine is placed first, it is heard because it comes first and the masculine is heard because it is perceived as the base form. I wrote an editorial that was twice published titled "Why We Should Say 'Women and Men' Until

It Doesn't Matter Any More,"[16] the point being that until the sexes are no longer ranked, speaking in this fashion (which is perfectly possible in English) is one small way of helping to bring about a nonsexist world. It is quite surprising how much difference it can make, and how difficult it can be at the beginning, and how often editors/teachers will change what you have written: women and men, girls and boys, she and he, Eve and Adam, etc. Try it. I'd love to hear how it goes for you.

Conclusion

In this essay what may be new vocabulary (unless you've been around me) forms *the* important item: naming is the first step to handling anything:

Derivational thinking

Number

Sex-based derivation

Ranking

Cheswam

Russ Categories

Denial of agency

Pollution of agency

False categorization

Isolation

Anomalousness

Passive exonerative

I also affirm the importance of two concepts that don't require a new vocabulary, merely new modes of thought: recognizing a lack of models, and placing the feminine first in ordered items.

Now a request: like the assignment I give my students and workshop participants, it would be delightful if you-all would listen during WisCon for examples of the Russ Categories as they apply to women and minorities, and send them to me at hardman@ufl.edu, or to the editor of this volume at nisis@aol.com. Should the editor of the next WisCon Chronicles agree, we could publish them; if not I would certainly find them useful. More importantly, as we change our language in our talking journey towards the realization of our ideology, we also help along the journey towards the changing of our culture to the realization of our ideology. May we journey together in fun, talk, and joy as we make the language we use all day every day that which we wish to live.

Endnotes

1.   Two translations, neither of which quite catch the flavor:
     Trans. Abel Alves, Carol Blakney

     "Misguided men, who will chastise/
     a woman when no blame is due,/
     oblivious that it is you/
     who prompted what you criticize...."

     Trans. Alan S. Trueblood

     You Men (English)
     Silly, you men-so very adept
     at wrongly faulting womankind,
     not seeing you're alone to blame
     for faults you plant in woman's mind.

2.   1648 ~1651-1695

3.   Hardman, MJ. "Linguistic Postulates and Applied Anthropological Linguistics," in *Papers on Linguistics and Child Language Ruth Hirsch Weir Memorial Volume*, Honsa and Hardman, eds., 1978, Mouton, The Hague.

4.   Hardman, MJ. "Postulados Linguisticos del Idioma Aymara," in *Reto del Multilinguismo en el Perú*, Alberto Escobar, ed., 1972, IEP, Lima, Perú.

5.   Hardman, MJ. "Linguistic Postulates and Applied Anthropological Linguistics," in *Papers on Linguistics and Child Language Ruth Hirsch Weir Memorial Volume*, Honsa and Hardman, eds., 1978, Mouton, The Hague.

6.   This one deserves its own story, not here, but someday.

7.   A clarification here on the nature of language, particularly appropriate to SF and part of why I have been so drawn to SF:

1) It is true that you can say **anything** in **any** language.

2) It is true that everything can be translated.

3) It is true that nothing can be translated.

These last two look like contradictions. They are not. The Italians have a saying < *traduttore, traditore* >, the translator is a traitor. The very best translation will evoke in the second audience the same emotional reaction to the document as the first. The ability to do this is rare. In all translations we get more than was there and less than was there by the very nature of language. For that reason translation is simultaneously an art and a science and a recreation. If any of you have read a work in its translation and also in its original language you will know what I mean.

4) It is true that completely accurate translation is not possible.

5) It is true that some things are said easily in some languages and that they are very difficult in other languages.

As Edward Sapir said <No two languages are ever sufficiently similar to be considered as representing the same social reality. The worlds in which different societies live are distinct worlds, not merely the same world with different labels attached.> [Sapir, Edward (1929), "The status of linguistics as a science," *Language* 5] For example, in English you **must** indicate number, and therefore you notice always then number of things, whether singular or not; in Jaqaru that is irrelevant—what you **must** notice is where you got the information you are sharing: from the language of someone else (or a book), from personal experience, or from history where no one is still alive or a story from long ago (non-personal knowledge).

The big difference between languages is not what you **can** say but what you **must** say—which is why translations always omit and add information that was/was not in the original.

8.   This paragraph, material in the CHESWAM paragraph, and much of the material in the actual discussion of the Russ Categories is taken, sometimes verbatim, from the text *Making the Invisible Visible*, forthcoming e-book by MJ Hardman and Anita Taylor, designed by Catherine Wright, with permission.

9.   Russ, Joanna. University of Texas. 1983. ISBN 0292724454.

10. Just in case you missed that:

GLOTOLOG, n., stand. Intergalactic, current:

Dominant sapients Tau Ceti 8

...

Dispar 2.

GLOTOLOG, n., colloq. Intergalactic, current:

Information control without direct censorship.

Prologue *How to Suppress Women's Writing.* Russ, Joanna. University of Texas. 1983. [If you don't know what is omitted by...you have a real treat awaiting you; it should be required reading for every SF fan].

11. Hardman, MJ 1994 "Observations for Language and Gender Courses Using Joanna Russ," Women and Language 17:2

12. Taking into consideration all of the material in *Making the Invisible Visible*, forthcoming e-book by MJ Hardman and Anita Taylor, designed by Catherine Wright.

13. Even so, when we were married in New York State, it was still illegal for us to do so across the line in New Jersey. What we, and our children, have experienced is also a very long and interesting story, but not now.

14. See Chapter Four of *Making the Invisible Visible*, forthcoming e-book by MJ Hardman and Anita Taylor, designed by Catherine Wright.

15. The most recent set is:

America's Women: Four Hundred Years of Dolls, Drudges, Helpmates, and Heroines by Colins Gail

Her Story: A Timeline of Women Who Changed America by Charlotte S. Waisman and Jill S. Tietjen

History of Women in the Sciences: Readings from Isis by Sally Gregory Kohlstedt

Mothers of Invention: From the Bra to the Bomb, Forgotten Women and Their Ideas by Ehlie Ann Vare and Greg Ptacek

Women into the Unknown: A Sourcebook on Women Explorers and Travelers by Marion Tinling

Women of Discovery: A Celebration of Intrepid Women Who Explored the World by Milbry Polk and Mary Tiegreen

Women Without Superstition: "No Gods-No Masters." The Collected Writings of Women Freethinkerss of the Nineteenth and Twentieth Centuries by Annie Laurie Gaylor.

But there are so many, many more out there that they are no longer confined to the syllabus list; it is only a place to start. They are still charged with finding someone they have never heard of, but would have liked to have heard of, either a POC or a woman.

16. 1999 "Why we should say 'women and men'" until it doesn't matter any more," *Women and Language* 22:1 Spring 1999;

Guest Editorial, pp 1-2 and 1999 "Why we should say 'women and men' until it doesn't matter any more," Free Mind November/December as Guest Editorial p. 3.

Editor's Note:

> As *The WisCon Chronicles* goes to press, we all mourn the recent death of Joanna Russ, originator of the categories MJ Hardman uses and expands upon in this work. MJ has told me how deeply it saddens her that Joanna will never see this particular legacy of her thoughts and writing. Joanna's legacies are many, rich, and, we hope, long-lasting.

Racial Identity and Writing — Part Two

edited by Eileen Gunn

Do you consider racial and cultural issues when you write? How? Why or why not?

Claire Light: Yes. Because that's what I live, that's what I see, and that's how I think.

Nick Mamatas: Of course. Partially for the reasons I mentioned earlier, partially because the US (where most of my work is set) was built on racism—on both slavery and the genocide of the indigenous population. I'm also Greek (I don't like the term "Greek-American," and for the most part, in my experience, Greeks don't use that term, either here or in Greece—but I was born in the US) and write a lot about Greeks in America and issues of assimilation, modernity, and being "of two worlds."

Yoon Ha Lee: It depends on the story. I like writing stories that draw on Korean or other East Asian folklore and imagery, but they don't necessarily address particular issues. Sometimes the issues are front and center. My story "Ghostweight" recently appeared in *Clarkesworld*, and while the setting is not Korean (it takes place in a secondary world), it is concerned with genocide and cultural assimilation; I was thinking of the Japanese occupation when I wrote it.

Gavin Grant: Yes. I know my own story, I'm interested in exploring it a little, but more so other people's stories—mostly on this planet (I haven't written much off/other-planet fiction). Everyone should go live abroad sometime, as it really underlines how universal some things are (i.e., everyone eats) and how *differently* everyone does these things.

Ben Rosenbaum: Sure, as much as I can. One writes about people, after all, and people are made of culture.

I think the only story that engages directly head-on with nowadays, US-American concepts of race is "Stray," co-written with David Ackert, who is Iranian-American and, like me, somewhat racially ambiguous. I didn't find out until college that he didn't think of himself as white; so it's perhaps no surprise that that story features a racially liminal figure, an immortal so masterful at fitting the expectations of those around him that he tries to navigate the segregated South being black at some times and white at others. This doesn't work out so well for him. Racism and colonialization are also central to "The Valley of Giants" (not always so well handled, there, alas) and "Orphans," for instance....

"Cultural issues" is of course a much broader category, and lots of my stories are Jewish stories— "The Book of Jashar," "The City of Peace," "Biographical Notes to 'A Discourse on the Nature of Causality, with Airplanes'"....

Mark Rich: To some degree, always—or never. It comes to mind that in writing one of my *Analog* stories I saw, in my mind's eye, the characters as mostly of one "race," while giving them names drawn from a different ethnic background. Neither one was Anglo-Swiss or Japanese. Am I always blurring matters in this way? I wonder, sometimes.

In writing *C.M. Kornbluth: The Life and Works of a Science Fiction Visionary*, however, I can say that the racial-cultural aspects of the story were almost constantly present in mind—at least in the final stages, as I grew increasingly aware of their importance.

Andrea Hairston: See my answer to the first question. I don't quite know what you mean by issues. Problems? Questions? Challenges? I think of a statement by Senegalese poet and former president Leopold Senghor, "I feel the Other, I dance the Other, therefore I am." My central concerns are cultural. How do we make meaning? How do we conjure the world we want?

Doselle Young: Building upon what I've already said, the gut response remains overwhelmingly negative because, while they can certainly be interesting (and relevant to the human condition in general), racial and cultural issues, no matter what the specifics, will always have their roots firmly planted in our evolutionary and biological pasts, and to examine these issues without taking that into account seems rather lazy to me or, at the least, almost criminally short-sighted.

It must be said that I don't use the word "criminal" lightly. I believe that writers (particularly writers of science fiction) have a unique responsibility to not only take part in, but to also elevate the level of social discourse and, while it's impossible to know exactly what effects an understanding of the roles both evolutionary biology and cognitive science play in how racial and cultural issues manifest themselves, I can only imagine that to do so would do more good than harm. Might afford us human beings an increased ability to remember that, no matter how personal such issues (whatever the specifics) might feel, their causes are most often, at heart, far more than merely historical.

In short, "racial and cultural issues" hold little interest for me beyond their usefulness in illustrating or revealing some aspect of overall human nature—the quantum mechanics of the human animal.

Think: fiction as cognitive and evolutionary archeology.

Perhaps it's a matter of semantics but, in my view, it's not as if any of us can really claim ownership of a culture or of our cultural experiences *per se*. We can only report upon our individual historical inheritance. We can outline our intimate familiarity with that inheritance: survey our emotional connections (positive, negative, or otherwise) to our inheritance, illuminate our desire to belong and/or the social pressures exerted by others for us to identify and conform to any particular group. If we can do all this and acknowledge the powerful role that the observations of other people play in our sense of self (or that of whatever characters we've chosen to write about), then I'd say we're on the right track.

Stories Matter

by Nancy Jane Moore

When people who hold filmmakers to a high standard criticize the inaccuracies in science fiction epics and television shows, the defense is swift: "It's just entertainment," we are told. With science fiction and fantasy novels and short stories, the response is a condescending "That's just genre fiction." It's not even worthy of reviews in serious publications; why would anyone care if the author got things very wrong?

In fact, some people dismiss any fiction as frivolous. The idea that something is "just a story" or "just a movie" and therefore unimportant is widespread.

Yet even those who pooh-pooh some or all fiction must be aware that lots of people see the movies, watch the TV shows, and even read the books. Perhaps the high-minded intellectual elite who dismiss science fiction out of hand can keep all the information they take in carefully compartmentalized in their brains — this bit came from "entertainment" or "genre" and therefore shouldn't be taken seriously, while this idea from "real literature" should be remembered — but I doubt most people have such a clear mental filing system. Ideas get jumbled together, and sources fall by the wayside.

Those jumbled ideas create our understanding of the world. If the information in movies and stories contains half-truths and stereotypes, we will end up with an inaccurate understanding of what is going on. There are also people deliberately disseminating misinformation, and telling stories that distort truth in the name of entertainment just adds more ignorance to the mix.

At WisCon 34, Andrea Hairston made this point clearly with a devastating (and highly entertaining) critique of the movie *District 9*. It included a brilliant explanation of how satire can misfire and be misunderstood: If you mock a culture that most of the audience only knows vaguely and stereotypically—as *District 9* does with Nigerians—you simply perpetuate the stereotype. Satire requires that the audience know the whole truth; otherwise, they don't get the joke and treat humorous exaggeration as fact.

But the thing Hairston said that really got my attention was her response to the repeated defense of *District 9* as "only entertainment": "Who does it serve if we believe that the stories we tell ourselves are insignificant?" I immediately grabbed a pen and wrote that question down, and I've been thinking about it ever since.

I worked it into my own presentation at that WisCon—"A Path to Ending Women's Fear of Men"—because it added depth to my thoughts on the importance of getting women warriors right even in the most lightweight of adventure stories.

I'm not yet sure who it serves if most storytelling is dismissed as insignificant—those wedded to the status quo, perhaps, or those who don't want to devote time and energy to creating a substantive story to go along with the bells and whistles on their blockbuster movies. (Yes, I'm talking about *Avatar* here.) As Hairston said in her presentation, "Longer paper."

But I do know who it *harms* if we consider our stories insignificant: Everyone who creates stories or consumes them.

What is that harm? A lack of true understanding of the depth and richness of the world around us. If we don't respect what we read and view, we will never learn to distinguish between a real human being—a complex mess of virtues and shortcomings capable of great heroism and shocking stupidity—and the stereotype of the evil dictator, the whore with the heart of gold, or the lone hero. How can we recognize the danger posed by the person motivated by good intentions if we think evil laughs like a melodrama villain, or act heroically if we think that's a role reserved for perfect individuals who need no one else?

Writers who buy into the idea that stories are insignificant will not make the effort (and it is hard work) to meld understanding of the world around them with imagination to produce the larger truths. Worse, they will begin to consider their own work meaningless. Treating stories as insignificant cheapens life for us all.

I believe in fiction. In fact, I wrote an essay about it that was featured on a local radio station when NPR was running its "This I Believe" series. I said, "[W]hen it comes to understanding what life is all about, imagination trumps fact." I'm very serious about this, which is why I don't like to hear writers say they lie for a living. Sure, writers make things up—we're supposed to make things up—but it is by this exercise of our imagination that we get to real truth. "Just the facts, ma'am," rarely tells an honest story. Or a whole one.

One of David Weber's Honor Harrington books was offered at the Tiptree auction at WisCon. I had to sit on my hands to keep from making a negative bid along the lines of "Pay me $25 to take this junk off your hands." Of course, the purpose of the auction is to raise money, not make political commentary on the objects being sold, but the Honor Harrington stories are so completely at odds with the purpose of the Tiptree that it was hard not to mock them.

Why do I think these books about a female military hero are inappropriate items for the Tiptree auction? Despite the female hero and the fact that the books are set quite some distance in the future, the gender relationships of this society are virtually indistinguishable from those of the present day. Here's the message I get from those books: Gender is set in stone, and even in a future where a woman can become a major military leader, her mother is still worrying about when she's getting married.

I'm way past the point of cheering for a character just because I'm told she's a warrior, especially if the author doesn't understand basic things about warriorship. A character who solves every problem by slugging someone is not much of a warrior. Nor is someone who kills people without being affected by it.

Gwyneth Jones explained this problem clearly in the "Shora Revisited" essay in her nonfiction collection *Imagination/Space* (Aqueduct Press, 2009):

> The nineties saw the rise of sf feminism for a larger group, if not for the masses: a rationale and a canon of texts for men and women who wanted to see themselves as 'feminists' but who at heart remained ordinary sf punters. They didn't want the violence to be real or the truths to be inconvenient. They wanted feel-good science fiction, as before, just with women in the starring roles and essentially feminine values celebrated. (p. 60)

There was a time in my life when I would have been satisfied, as a writer and as a reader, with simple adventure stories starring tough women. I spent far too much of my childhood identifying with male heroes because there weren't any stories about women warriors out there. I was hungry for stories in which women got to have all the fun, instead of being the brief love interest or the person who wailed, "Do you have to go out and fight?" (I cannot adequately express my distaste for the constantly repeated story convention in which the hero's wife or girlfriend urges him to give up his principles and run.)

But that time has passed. Now if you give me a story with an "exceptional" woman or one with a woman who is channeling the classic tough-as-nails Marine drill sergeant, you're going to bore me and probably make me angry, because those are stereotypes, and like most stereotypes, they're highly inaccurate. And I know this firsthand.

I've spent 31 years in the martial arts, so I know a lot of people who study the way of warriorship. They come in a variety of sizes, shapes, personalities, ages, and genders. What they share in common is an ability to read situations and a willingness to put themselves on the line when things get very bad. Some like to project the tough image, though that's the kind of thing that tends to fade away with age and experience.

But the other reason I have no patience with the exceptional woman or the one who is tough-as-nails—the woman who is "just like a man"— is that when I was young and trying to figure out my own path in life, I thought that was who I had to be if I wanted to be anything more than "just a housewife," the fate prescribed for me by the stories I read, the culture around me, and specifically by my high school history teacher when I mentioned my thoughts about law school. (It could be I stayed in law school just because I'd been told I couldn't do it. I wasn't going to wimp out like a girl.)

The stereotype taught me my only chance at something other than housewifery was to become exceptional in a male-like way. It took me some years to figure out there were other ways to become a powerful actor in the world than taking on the equally stereotypical role of the male hero. Some of that truth I gleaned by acting in the world, some I learned through the study of Aikido, but a lot of it came from reading stories that expanded my thinking and showed me other avenues.

What is true of gender is also true of race and culture. Uhura on *Star Trek* provided welcome relief for both women and people of color in the 1960s, but such tokenism is unlikely to move us, or help us, today. (Her role was expanded somewhat in the recent *Star Trek: Enterprise*, though a movie that begins with that hoariest of clichés, a woman giving birth in the middle of a battle, is hardly a good example of how far we've come. A few centuries in the future and there are still no decent family leave policies for people about to become parents?)

Things have moved on from the milieu of the original *Star Trek*, though images of African Americans in popular culture still tend to be either street hustlers or nurturing people who take much better care of their white friends than those friends deserve. Neither image is an accurate depiction of the African Americans I know, who—like all the other people I know—tend to not fit into neat little compartments of ready-made roles.

But stereotypes are easier, and gangsters and saints both make good movie subjects. After all it's "just entertainment." And so the false images take hold. Add in the modern convention that the darker and grittier a story is, the truer it is, and it's easy for people to believe that the only real stories about African Americans are the violent ones about gangsters, drugs, and murder.

It is easier to see past the stereotypes when you know the people being typecast. I am not likely to believe one mean redneck stands in for all of them, or one greedy lawyer indicts the whole profession. And I assuredly don't believe the stereotype of high-maintenance women out to take men for every dime they've got. Even if the stereotype has been done to death, if you really know the people being typecast, you know the truth.

But what happens when you don't know much about the people in the story, when your only knowledge of, say, Nigerians comes from a couple of newspaper headlines and a movie like *District 9*? It's so easy simply to believe the stories are true.

Criticism can help fight the poorly-conceived and stereotypical stories out there, but there's another cure: Good stories that don't fall into those traps.

WisCon to the rescue: It introduced me to the work of Nnedi Okorafor.

I'm not very knowledgeable about Africa. I've had a little exposure to Zulu culture from a workshop I once took, heard my father's World War II stories about North Africa, read some of Doris Lessing's fiction set in what is now Zimbabwe, and seen a lot of news reports about war, genocide, famine, and corruption. I know about colonialism and apartheid, but I don't know all the stories in all the places. And my sense of African geography is lousy, since the last time anybody bothered to teach me anything about Africa I was in the seventh grade. It has changed since then.

Okorafor writes stories that blend science fiction and fantasy and sets them in African lands. And while her work does not give me any "facts" about what these places are like in the present day (because, as a good writer, she exercised her imagination) they do give me a sense of African people surviving in a difficult world, and of the kind of stories and myths they might invent.

These stories do not include a European or American hero who comes in and shows the simple tribal people the truth of their culture. They are about African people—in *The Shadow Speaker*, for instance, a girl from Niger and a boy from Nigeria—who take action in the world to save it. These are not perfect people, and she does not paint a paradise; even the wise among her characters sometimes do a foolish thing, and the world has slavery and other evils.

But while Okorafor has not written "realistic" novels that would remedy my weak African geography and history, she has given me a deeper sense of people and place than any list of facts could provide. That is, by providing a new perspective, particularly by introducing me to a world in which African people solve their own problems, she has changed my view of the world a little.

That is what stories are supposed to do. And why they matter.

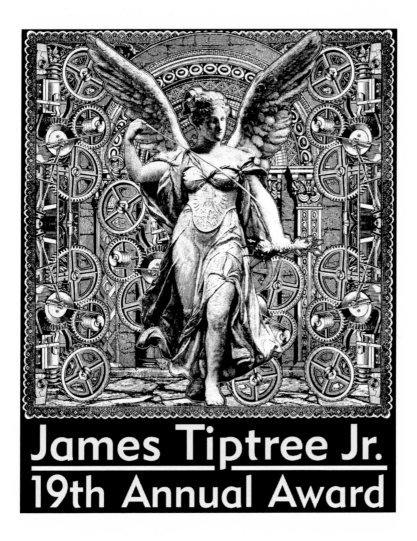

James Tiptree Jr.
19th Annual Award

James Tiptree, Jr. Award art courtesy of Freddie Baer

2010 Tiptree Award Acceptance Speech on behalf of Fumi Yoshinaga

by Mari Kotani
(Chair, The Japanese Association of Gender Fantasy and Science Fiction)

Let me start by reading a very short message from Ms. Fumi Yoshinaga, the author of *Ōoku: The Inner Chambers.*

Many thanks for giving me this year's Tiptree Award. *Ōoku: The Inner Chambers* is intended to be a manga work that comes under the heading of light entertainment. Therefore, the news of its winning this prestigious award first embarrassed me, and then humbled me, but finally gratified me very deeply.

In retrospect, I have to confess that when I began writing *Ōoku*, I couldn't know if this work would be successful in Japan. At that point, I didn't expect it to be translated into other languages. Now that I am informed that the members of the Tiptree Award committee fully enjoyed reading my work in the United States, I feel absolutely delighted.

The first two volumes of *Ōoku*, which the Tiptree committee very generously appreciated, are only the beginning of the story. Keenly conscious of the prestige of the Tiptree Award, I'm obliged to complete the whole narrative. If you read through all the volumes of *Ōoku* when it is completed, I would be very pleased. Thank you very, very much!!!

As you all know, *Ōoku: the Inner Chambers* already received, in 2005, the Sense of Gender Award, the Japanese version of Tiptree Award organized by our group, The Japanese Association of Gender Fantasy and Science Fiction. The ceremony took place at the 45th Japanese National Convention of Science Fiction held on July 9th in Matsushima, Miyagi Prefecture, and the winner received a special trophy and a folding fan, "sensu" in Japanese, which is a pun on "sense" of gender.

For your information, I would like to tell you what happened at the meeting of our judging committee. To put it simply, all the judges understood that gender-bending in *Ōoku* is incredibly complicated. For example, sociologist Tomomi Shibuya said the fictionality of *Ōoku* illuminates the very fictionality of our own reality. Poet Yumio Sato closely compared *Ōoku* with Sally Potter's film adaptation of Virginia Woolf's novel *Orlando*, and concluded that both works, through their intelligent strategy for gender bending, do not intend simple retaliation against traditional patriarchy but speculate on the complexity of gender politics. Pornography critic Kaoru Nagayama admired erotic aspects of the work, giving an insight into the eroticism of politics as well as the politics of eroticism. Furthermore, web designer Min Onouchi analyzes the hidden agenda of "true name" in *Ōoku* as closely related with the tradition of fantasy.

We Japanese feminists are deeply interested to know the way *Ōoku* has been accepted internationally. The good news is that the author, Fumi Yoshinaga, still keeps writing this work. I look forward to having an opportunity to further develop our transpacific discussion on *Ōoku* in the near future.

Thank you for your attention.

Mari Kotani accepts the Tiptree Award for Volume 1 of *Ōoku: the Inner Chambers* on behalf of Fumi Yoshinaga.

Excerpt from
Ōoku: The Inner Chambers

by Fumi Yoshinaga

13

Courtesy of Fumi Yoshinaga and Hakusenska, Inc.

And so it was that close to eighty years passed...

Because its symptoms resembled those of smallpox, the disease came to be called the Redface Pox. And, with no effective cure for it ever found, it took root as a horrible, yet common, disease.

Trades and occupations that had been passed down from father to son were now handed down from mother to daughter.

...and, due to their alarmingly low survival rate, boys were raised with extreme care as precious seed-bearers, with all the labor in the land carried out by women.

The male population of the country stabilized at about one-fourth that of the female...

The institution of marriage collapsed. Low-income women could not even dream of taking a husband, so they visited the pleasure districts and paid for men's favors in order to bear children.

The right to take a son-in-law became a privilege accorded only the samurai warrior class and very wealthy merchants and village magistrates.

OH, I ENVY YOU, O-KAYA! HOW LUCKY YOU ARE THAT YOUR FAMILY'S TRADE GOES SO WELL.

PRITHEE HEAR MY NEWS—I MIGHT BE ABLE TO TAKE A BRIDEGROOM SOON!

YOUR HIGHNESS.

THEY AWAIT YOUR ENTRANCE.

HMM.

The sixth Tokugawa shogun, Ienobu.

Since samurai society in the peaceful years of the Tokugawa reign was already largely a bureaucracy, the inversion of men's and women's roles took place relatively smoothly.

Ever since the reign of the third shogun, Iemitsu, military rule of the country had also become a responsibility handed down from woman to woman.

Greer Gilman displays the antique music box presented to her as winner of the 2010 Tiptree Award for *Cloud & Ashes*.

Greer Gilman's Tiptree Thanks

Wow.

This breaks the White Queen's rule. Sometimes it really is jam today.

Dear goddesses of earth and air, I have a Tiptree!

And shared with Yoshinaga *sensei*—a marvellous and unexpected pairing. I am honored.

I began *Cloud & Ashes* on a typewriter, almost twenty years ago. Who knew it was radical?

Well, maybe it is. Not as a future but an otherwise, a lefthand world, in which men must be possessed by goddesses to act, and women turn the sky.

Mostly, people notice my extravagant language—my archeolinguistics. (I like to say that I do everything James Joyce did, only backwards and in high heels.) It's new and exhilarating for me to be read for my ideas, for the world the words make. I love that in one book I can have both recombinant balladry and Tiptree feminism, that I can be gender-bent in Jacobean iambics—hey, the Jacobeans were—that I can play with time paradoxes in full poetic drag, like an astrophysicist in an Erté gown. I can use ceremonial language as Elizabeth I used dress—as Quentin Crisp did in *Orlando*—as a form of intrinsic female power. As a spell.

This book has been so very fortunate in the godmothers at its cradle:

I'd like to thank my brilliant and importunate first readers, all of them.

Above all, my three of the Nine: Deb Manning, the goddess of fractally evolving fiction; Sonya Taaffe, who enticed me to the underworld (sadly, she could not be here at WisCon); and Lila Garrott-Wejksnora, of the archipelago of index cards.

Thank you, Faye Ringel, for auld lang syne.

Loving thanks to my mother, who went to Breadloaf in the '40s, who nearly went to Hollywood to write her screenplays, who married and had children and worked. I wish we could have seen her movies, read her books.

Thanks to my teachers: Barbara Whitesides, who let me just write, and Sylvia Adamson, who taught me to read, to analyze, and how language has evolved through time.

I'd like to thank Anon for all her ballads.

I'd like to remember the late miraculous Lal Waterson for her song, "The Scarecrow."

All hail to Kelly Link and Gavin Grant of Small Beer Press for venturing on so odd a book as mine. They have made it beautiful, within and out. I am overjoyed to bring them honor.

Love to Ursula, who loves her books to pieces.

Thank you, Motherboard and jury.

And thank you, friends.

Greer Gilman

Interior of the antique music box presented to
Greer Gilman for winning the 2010 Tiptree Award

On *Cloud & Ashes*

by Greer Gilman

Cloud is the world and Ashes is a Goddess there, the mirror-self and daughter of the chthonic Annis. Like an anti-Persephone, she's dark-born, amorous of light. She escapes from her mother's Law, the underworld, each spring, and every winter is snatched back. But her Cloud-returning wakes the earth, brings green and flowering out of winter dark. Spring is fugitive but autumn's endless: the Unleaving. It is both a *here* and *now*, a timeless fall; its god is the woodland spirit Tom o Cloud. He and Ashes and the winter-braving Witches—all these gods—are constellations: Cloudish myth is written in the sky.

At Lightfast, in midwinter, the Sun is in Ashes. In myth, she takes the dead Sun in her lap—her lover and her son—and wakes him. He arises. Everywhere in Cloud, his death and his rebirth are re-enacted in that season, in all manner of plays, from the roughest of guisings to the courtliest of masques. It is playing, in their world, which turns the sky. The guisers truly wake the sun, bring Ashes from her winter grave. They dance so the year is.

In these scenes from *Cloud & Ashes,* it is Lightfast now. A company of players gives a masque before a Cloudish household. Like the Jacobean players I spoke of in my Tiptree thanks, they are all men and boys; unlike them, these journeymen are something else: initiates in a mystery cult, possessed by what they play. Being otherwise than men, both more and less, they're held in awe while in *persona,* and in some contempt off-stage. The piece they're acting is a version of an ancient Cloudish myth (which some of you may know from *Moonwise*).

Two children of the house are watching from behind a curtain: Noll, the heir of Low Askwith, who is five, and his mother's younger sister Annot, just fifteen. They have a secret.

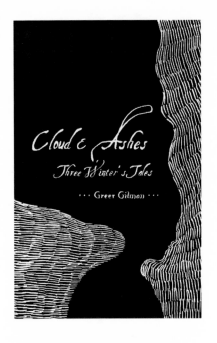

Excerpt from
Cloud & Ashes

~

...there come twa witches out o Lune...

In come the Witches—Rianty and Silvry—in their mantles of the sky, nightblue and starry. Scarves of silvery gauze are at their shoulders, wafting as they turn.

O brave, says Annot in his ear. *They've come by the Lyke Road, and they trail it.*

Are they women?

Goddesses.

Noll puzzles. They are maidenlike; yet wear bright swords and bucklers. Witchery, he thinks: for naked they are boys. Or so his nurse hath said. Their coats bespell them.

They've lanterns, he says.

They're lating Ashes, who is yet to come. Hush now, they speak their argument.

The world is winterfast, and they will turn it. Annot's told that play to him; has acted it, all voices, in her room. He will remember when he reads the verses, later, later. He will weep. Now what he hears of it is music, fitfully, in gusts: a wind full of whirling leaves, a wild confusion. Some words he leaps at, snatches from the air; most others oversail him.

Now they've gone aside.

Here's Tom o Cloud shivering in the snow. He stamps and blows his nail. He's bristled like an urchin's back beneath a load of eldins. *Kin kindling*, he calls it. He is wood; his words are strange. The witches enter and amaze him; he amuses them. *His dreams do prick him and he flowers*. Annot's laughing at poor Tom, so Noll laughs too, uncertainly. As if their breath would blow him out. He's like a candleflame that burns the brighter for the wind that threatens. He might snuff.

They three will break the winter: they have sworn.

So now they journey in imagined snow. A man you're not to note sweeps back the rushes, laying bare the flags. The ground's chalked out as riddlestones, as islands in abyss. The ground's bewitched: for what is drawn is chasm. Where they've walked a moment since is fathomless. A cold wind wuthers up from it. Earth gapes for them, and they must cross. Beyond is Law.

An hollow music plays, as if the earth's voice spoke.

They dance the Riddles. Leaping cross and cross them, in a crouch of terror: stone to stone. Noll watches in an ecstasy of fear. A stumble, and they'd fall forever. He can see them, even open-eyed: the black ice of the bodies and the cold white fire streaming upward like a comet's tail. They cannot win the brink. And then another music interweaves: a net of fiddle under over fiddle. It sustains. Now Tom o Cloud uncurls like bracken; now the witches dance the wilder, and the outswing of their lanterns traces fire in the air. They leap his staff, they tumble backward. He dances leaf light and askew: should fall. He never does. The wind that scatters raises him; the wind is story.

≋

A cold blast quells the fire.

Here is Law; and everywhere is Annis. Now, nowhere, anywhere: she plays like lightning on the fells. Her black hair fills the room like wind, like night; the candles crouch and flare.

Noll is trembling. Annot whispers, *Will I take thee out?*

I want to see.

She colls him; she is glad of his small warmth.

Now comes the slender music of the Cloudwood, like a pattering of rain, and then the twining of the Sisters' viols. Enter three champions. Annot gazes on the brown girl, the witch boy, half in love. In moving, she is perfectness, that still is sullen and farouche. A tarnished Silvry.

Here is Law, says Tom o Cloud. *I would be elsewhere, were it on a sinking ship, atwixt a bear and honey.*

Is the sorceress not here?

And happen at her book. I would not for the moon disturb her.

We are come to her undoing.

Turn and turn, the sisters call her down:

> By the elding of the moon
> By the weird of night and noon
> That foul or fair befall
> By the heavens' rime and rune
> I conjure you. I call.

Down from the fellside in a shock of winter strides Black Annis. She may take what shape she wills; goes now in a witch's like: not dwindled but distilled. The little sun is leashed before her, crouching, like a fire slaked with ash. His mistress wears a crown of souls, like hailstorm, and her very bones are moon.

Ah, breathes Annot. This is marvellous. No bloodnailed hag disfigured on a ballad sheet; nor yet an old wives' tale, a bugbear to affright the children. No grisly ghost, that stamping on the floor cries out, *more meat!* This witch is beautiful as frost is, fair and fell. Sheer deity.

Unmasked.

They say a man-witch dances Annis; but no man's throat was ever white as blackthorn, nor his wrist and hand so fine. They say that it's a woman bred to it in dark, that knows no living tongue. That in her secrets, she is neither. Of no mortal kind: a spirit summoned or a waft. The same witch always, anywhere, at once. Herself: for in devouring the mask becomes her.

Who calls me to the dance?

Three journeymen.

And I the mistress. Will you gage?

For the turning of the sun, we will.

This lateworm? What, this lowling? This catchfire gendered on a heap of punk? This Ashes-lap? He crouches at my lady's feet, his glory dimmed.

A golden lad that was, and come to this: a chimneysweeper. She could huff and he would scatter. *Tinsel. But your wager is souls.* She touches him, as if she sains him. *Eyes, mouth, heart: be stone.* Then she turns to the challenge. *I will dance the ay and O.*

Tom o Cloud stands forth. *I will dance the light of leaves.*

But he has not danced but a single dance, once round, when he is done. He whirls his staff at her, and through and through her like a mist. As good kill water with a knife: she slips him still, still-closing, woundless as a white hag rising from the moor. It whelms him. At a breath, he stands astounded, rooted in the earth. His arms, outflung as if to strike at her, outbranch; his leaves of tatters fall. His black staff flowers into frost and breaks. As frost will fell a tree, she fells him; he is winterslain.

Noll is stricken. Annot rocks him in her lap.

Hush, love. He will rise. I promise. As the sun will rise. With a dabbled napkin, she amends his face. *'Tis but a winter's tale. Look now, the sisters come to dance for him.*

So fleeting childish grief is: he is rainbow through his tears, he's rapt.

Two on one, they draw on her, at fence. They stand triskelion, a wheel of witches. Then the swords fall clanging to the earth.

His death was not the wager settled. Still I dance the ay and O.

The dark witch — Silvry, with her tarnished hair — stands forth. *I will dance the dayspring.*

Sunwise, thrice and thrice around she heels it, leap and landing, lightfoot to the drub of drum. At every turn she raises up her shield a little higher in its arc until — O heavens — she uplifts the Sun. It brightens, burning through the cataract of cloud: an ember at her heel, a shoulderknot of fire, a glory. How it blazes in her vault! It glitters in my lady's crown, like daybreak in a shattering of hail.

And Annis in a rage cries out: *Who slipped my sister that was bound? Who broached her?* Whirling, ranting, how she storms. Her great black sleeves fly out like raven's wings. *Who turned the glass that night may run? Who let her rune of blood to run? How came she lighter of a Sun?* Riddles, riddles. How she stamps it! How she ramps and rages, spurning with her heel.

Annot shivers. In the witch's fury she's recalled her grim aunt stalking from her sister's childbed, bare arms bloody to the shoulder. Three days crying out upon the moon, that would not lighten her. And then the still child in the bearing-cloth, as blue as lead. A girl. And yet again her sister breeds, will kindle ere the greening Ashes rises from the dark. *O my sister. She will rise from this. She must.*

The second witch stands forth.

I will dance the darklong, and the changes of the moon.

And moonwise, thrice and thrice around she heels it and uplifts the Moon. At every turn it changes, childing of itself. The riddle read: it is the gendering Moon that does, undoes the knot of blood in woman, and the Moon that lightens her; the Moon that goes with child of mutability. It rounds: is bright edged at the first, a bow new bent; and at the full, sheer silver to the brim. Night's glass.

My lady gazes. She is lost in admiration, in the mazes of the moon. She holds it as a mirror. And it seems another Annis gazes out at her. The one is all of night and silver; and the other bloodfast, hag and whore: her shadow self, outrooted and despised. They draw each other in the glass. They meddle; they are gone. The glass lies empty on the ground.

The witches lift it up, exulting. In it is the sky in little, flawless: sun, moon, stars, and all. A swirl of silver for the Road. All incrystalled in the glass, and still as frostwork on a pane. Down they cast the mirrorworld. It shatters, scattering across the floor like hailstones.

Gleefully, the household scrambles for the shards of Annis; but their garner melts away. 'Twas painted on a round of ice.

And the Sun, the burning boy, uprises. Doffs his coat for cloth of tinsel. But the tree—poor Tom—is leafless still, lies earthfast.

Get him up, cries Noll in agony. *She's dead now.*

As if she's heard, the light witch beckons to the Sun. *Wake him: for his dream is done. We played it.* And he sings the morning.

So Tom o Cloud rises up in green, unfolds: like an imp from an acorn, like a catkin from a hazel twig. Shakes out his rags that lie about him like a drift of last year's leaves. He catches up the bright Sun laughing, tosses him, high high up in the air. As high as the rooftree that is green with winter leaves. And there he seems to hang forever, ever falling, shining as the light reborn.

At the door-sill, Annot sets the garland on Noll's head. White buds like drops of milk. Of candlewax and ends of silk, he knows, just snippets; but she's wreathed the snow in it, she's made it real. A secret for his mammy. She parts the arras just a little on a glare and clamour. It is time now. He cannot. A wistful winding music plays. He will.

Now, she whispers. *Softly, softly.*

All in green, a green verge in her hand, the winter child arises from her mother's dark, walks barefoot through her shattered crown. But where she walks spring flowers.

He is Ashes and she keeps the year alive.

There's a hushing in the room, a susurration. Like a wind through branches, like a sea: the summertide. The winter leaves with her; she brings the green within, and *in* is not. No hall, no company, no fireside. A hill. At every step a green blade springs.

He carries Ashes in himself: he is a bowl for her, brim full of holiness. So he goes softly, lest she spill. And yet she overspills, and where the drops fall there are flowers. They are white, and rooted in the darkness. Ashes buds. He walks in wonderment.

But in the players' space, amid the dazing candles and the roar, she stumbles and he halts. Looks round and backward. All unwooded now. All faces. Annot?

And the witches who are not look shrewdly on him: would he fall?

He casts about him wildly. Annot?

There. She nods at him, encouraging: begin. But in her face the mischief and the pride have slipped a little, like his wreath. She's fretted for him now. *Don't turn round,* she's told him. *Keep on.* He's done it wrong.

And the dark witch calls, *Pray silence for my lady's imp.*

Confusion: what his legs know is a bow. The crowd of faces laugh, some not unkindly. And the Sun blears out his tongue. Crisis.

But Tom o Cloud lays a warm hand on his shoulder. Steady now. Then stepping back, he quirks a curtsey: half in homage and half prompt.

Later, ever after, he'll remember vividly: the whiff of eager sweat on sweat; how the brown of Tom o Cloud's face is crooked, paint askew on winter pallor; his smile. He'll dream of that: he will be standing at the verges of a greendark wood, afraid, afraid, and he will see it further in, run after. There and gone. Like flick of fire, a falling star. A wish.

But he is *she,* is Ashes now. Tom sets the garland straight.

Speak, lady. 'Tis your cue.

No part of his, unpracticed now: the words her own. She speaks her mother tongue, still milky with her draught of heaven.

> My mother got me in her glass.
> Still as snow on snow I pass;
> But green in greener world I wake
> And lighter of the dark I make.
> In my coming I do leave;
> Death of dying I bereave
> It's silent when she's done.

On the hillside is a door; beyond the door, a fire. On the sill there stands a girl in green to welcome Ashes in. She bids her.

Overcome with godhead suddenly, Noll turns and runs, he buries his head in his mother's not-now-lap, against her mystery. In that drumly hill is laid his sister yet unborn, who will be Ashes.

≫

Courtesy of Greer Gilman

On Divides, Boundaries, and *Distances*

by Vandana Singh

I remember telling Timmi Duchamp, editor of Aqueduct Press, that an earlier version of my novella *Distances* (Aqueduct, 2008) had elicited rather antagonistic responses from some male readers. I went on to explain that one of them had said somewhat grouchily that the protagonist didn't come across to him as a mathematician. Why would he say that? I asked her, rather naively. Timmi's response was, in effect: you have a *woman* solving a mathematical problem of galactic proportions, and she does it while immersed in a device called an *amnion*, and she can sense the mathematics of the world just by looking around her—what do you expect?

We talked a bit about how territorial so many men feel about mathematics and the sciences. Not all of them do—in my experience the men who identify as humanities types don't feel that way. Those who wish they had gone into science, or have to deal with science in their day jobs in an indirect or direct way, and have unexamined assumptions about how science is done, might feel uncomfortable at a female writer's unconventional portrayal of a scientist-mathematician. Certainly I hadn't deliberately planned to challenge their expectations—I am female, and a scientist as well as a writer, and the story of *Distances* seemed completely natural to me. I didn't see anything challenging about it until Timmi pointed out the possibilities. Unfortunately the story was challenging to one particular woman reader in a different way—she couldn't connect to the story *because* of the math/science in it. The response of the male readers puzzled me; this one made me sad.

I bring up these examples because they illustrate to me a problem about which I am deeply concerned: gendering in the sciences, which finds its way into the science fiction community as well. (For instance my impression is that far fewer women read or write [or better yet, redefine] hard SF or any SF in which the science is of central importance, compared to men.) In my research days I was a particle physicist, perhaps the most male chauvinist subculture of physics. I experienced firsthand how masculine, for lack of a better word, the field is—and by masculine I don't just mean that it is dominated by men, by often confrontational styles of interaction, and therefore culturally less welcoming to many women and some men. I mean that in the sciences, and particularly in my field, the approach itself is remote, reductionist, and impersonal in its delivery. I went into the sciences because science excited my sense of wonder and connection with the universe—yet what I met with in graduate school and later was an attitude that physicist Lee Smolin describes as "shut up and calculate," divorced from philosophy, ethics, context—you know, the big questions. I wasn't aware of anything but a vague disquiet, a sense of discomfort, while I was shutting up and calculating—it was only after ten years of distance from academia that I understood why. (Now that I am back as an assistant professor at a small university, I do engage with these issues in the classroom.)

So what I wanted to imagine in the world of *Distances* was a culture (actually two distinct cultures) in which the study of the harmonies of the world—what we'd call science and mathematics—was not separate from other things, and in fact was intimately tied to poetry, myth, religion, and the daily rhythms of existence. I've always been fascinated by the great metaphors implicit in science (science itself can be viewed as a very long and involved interweaving of metaphors, but that is a story for another day), and how easily scientific ideas lend themselves to myth-making; I've explored this in a couple of stories up at *Strange Horizons* as well. In *Distances* I run with all this further than I've done before.

In addition I wanted to bring out both the beauty of science and its potential for destruction. In particular, one of the cultures of the story views the application of science—what we'd call technology—with great suspicion, since to put sacred truths to mundane use is, according to them, to put the world in danger.

One hope I'd had with this story was to share with readers the aesthetic beauty of mathematics, to seduce them with language and myth. I know I failed with at least one female reader. And that's the other thing that deeply bothers me: the belief that so many women have that they can't do science and math. I recall the time when a very bright young female SF writer dismissed my attempt to explain how to use the time dilation formula for close-to-light-speed travel for her story. "It's just square roots," I told her, when she said she was bad at mathematics. I am afraid I turn into a zealot when told such things. But she said she couldn't deal with square roots, that she just wanted the answer. I couldn't convince her that the exercise was worth doing, and that she would understand it. I come up against this attitude again and again, in and out of the classroom.

Of course gender isn't the only issue in the sciences; race is another one. Race and gender and class intersect in myriad ways in the real world; in *Distances*, too, the protagonist, Anasuya, is of a visibly different race, living in a place far from home, where she experiences the kind of distancing familiar to those who are exoticized. Inevitably this influences her most intimate relationships. How do you love someone who is the Other? What do you see when you look at them? Is it possible to bridge the abyss that separates races and cultures? And what about economic or technological considerations? A person from a world eighteen light years away, beholding Anasuya and her talent, sees her and others like her as people to be used, exploited.

In early 2010 I heard that *Distances* had been named a Tiptree Honor book. This made me feel surprised, humbled, and thrilled all at once. I've read several stories by James Tiptree, Junior, as well as works by other writers who explore and transcend the boundaries that separate gender from gender, race from race, and culture from culture. I have to say that for me such transgressive works have a value beyond the academic one—for a writer who negotiates these boundaries every day in real life, they offer so much more. In nurturing the spirit and exciting the imagination they make it possible to go on from day to day in an often cruel world. Modern urban society separates us from each other through walls of wood and brick and custom—good literature brings down these walls and builds a community of people and ideas. To be part of that conversation, that community, is a privilege indeed.

So, *Distances*. Here is an excerpt from it that I hope gives an idea of the story, although the geography and the mood shifts from part to part. This extract describes how Anasuya finds her special talent, her *athmis*, awakening within her as a child.

Excerpt from *Distances*

Growing up on the sloping beaches of Sagara—amid the phal-
lic pneumetaphores of the marshgrove trees, on the slippery,
matted floors of the raft-islands—swimming in the green,
dappled light of the seaweed forest, she had always suspected
that there were hidden patterns underlying the variegated
splendor of the world. The athmis came alive in her while she
was swimming underwater between rafts on a perfect, ordinary day. Years later she could recall it with clarity: the feel of
salt water in her mouth and neck-slits, a singing in her veins
that made her prickle all over, and the new sense awakening
inside her like a window opening in a blank wall. Then the
sudden crescendo of mathematical harmonies in her mind,
as she floated in the marsh forest: in the fractal landscape,
a shimmering of sinusoidal disturbances as an eel swam by,
the delicate exponentiation evident in parthenogenic two-
fish birthing in the water, each daughter fish budding off two
more daughters before swimming away. Gazing at ripples
cross each other in ever expanding circles, she realized with a
rush of delight that the book of knowledge had opened to her,
revealing the secret relationships between things: the length
and undulation of waves and their speed, the height of a falling rock and the time it took to splash into the sea. The myriad geometries surrounding her became readily apparent:
the smooth swell of the waves, the hollows between them,
the dimpling of tiny whirlpools as the water swept between
the weeds. She had no names yet for so many things, but she
sensed the mathematics of the world as a young child knows
colors before it learns the words. The realization swept over
her that everything in the world was in constant conversation
with every other thing, that all was flux and play. Swimming in
the green and gold light, she knew she would never be alone
in such a world.

Courtesy of Vandana Singh

Racial Identity and Writing — Part Three

edited by Eileen Gunn

Depending on your race, do you see certain topics as being forbidden to you? Or obligatory?

Nick Mamatas: I don't feel that any topic is forbidden or obligatory, no.

Gavin Grant: No on both. Not everything fits every story (of mine, anyway—I know it will be different for others).

Claire Light: No, nothing forbidden. Yes, I'm obliged to dig past the overlay of existing narrative, find some element of unrecorded truth from life, and then shape a narrative to contain that. It doesn't necessarily have to be about race, but race informs so much of my truth that it very often is.

Yoon Ha Lee: I can't think of any topics that I'd consider obligatory. I would probably not be willing to write a story about how awesome Hideyoshi was, but I don't think it would necessarily be wrong for a Korean to write that story; it's just that I don't think I could go there.

Ben Rosenbaum: I'm not sure what forbidden and obligatory would mean; "obligatory" maybe in the sense of "morally incumbent upon me to explore?" But no, not really. You need to write what you need to write. "It is not required of us to finish the work, but nor are we free to desist from it."

Andrea Hairston: Writing is sacred play, at the edge of the conscious and unconscious. I feed my spirit, but the notion of directing it is laughable. Writing is a revelation—I might discover things that are forbidden or obligatory as I write, but I don't write with obligations or limits in mind.

Mark Rich: The histories of Japanese-Americans and Japan-USA relations are fraught with unpleasant episodes. Call them specters in the closet. Oddly enough, I almost always think I know too little about them to draw upon them in my writing. I suppose I feel they are forbidden to me unless I am to do them justice. I have no doubt that others have drawn upon these episodes in writing various bits of sentimental realism—not a valid option for me. I have, however, written a few minor encyclopedia entries on aspects of the Japanese-American story. (Which exercise underlined for me my insufficiency of knowledge.)

Doselle Young: No. I think there's a place in fiction to explore anything and everything. Full stop. I don't perceive anyone else as having either the right or authority to forbid me from writing about whatever topic resonates for me. More, I don't see myself as having anything to gain by being too concerned about whether any particular reader's feelings might be negatively impacted by what I've written, as long as what I've written exhibits a clear attention to detail and a relevant degree of forethought.

In short, then, I'd say: any writer should feel free to write whatever he or she wants.

It's just better not to get caught with your pants down.

WisCon, Stories, and Ontological Blackness

by Maurice Broaddus

One of the first things we are taught as writers is to write what we know. One of the first things that you learn as an artist is that your art is an exploration of truth. Sometimes the truth to be mined is your own inner journey. One of the major themes that comes out in my work is that of identity: who we are vs. who we're expected to be. I suspect the reason for this is my own attempt to explore my identity, heritage, and roots through my stories. This reason was something I hadn't really considered consciously before I attended WisCon for the first time in 2010. One of the panels, "Why are All the Black Kids Sitting Together in the Cafeteria," really struck home.

I'm a black nerd: a Dungeons & Dragons-playing, Magic: the Gathering-crushing, action-figures-still-in-their-original-packages, comic-book-loving, and occasional Dream-Theater-listening nerd. I've been thinking about some of the iterations of blackness. I know how so many folks, within and without of the black community, like to define blackness by some sort of standard of ghetto ethos. But what about those of us raised in a majority white environment, children of affirmative action and assimilation? The "exceptions?" The folks who get compliments like "You speak so well" or "You're a credit to the race." The ones who receive loving epithets like "Oreo," "Sell-out," or—if class gets mixed into the equation—"Bougie." Such barbs strike me as a reaction to the idea of betraying community, a term to keep us in line as we're policed by other Bougies projecting their black insecurities. The Blacker-than-thou crowd demonstrating their superiority by shaming us back. It's bad enough when I'm made to feel I don't live up to the idea of true blackness held by people inside the culture, but this name-calling can also come from those outside it (which always sounds to me like "you're not black like the hip hop guys I see on MTV"), which then borders on the ridiculous.

My mother was born in Jamaica. She traveled to London, England, when she entered nursing school. My US-born father met her there while he was in the Air Force; thus my British citizenship. When I was six years old, our family moved to the cosmopolitan metropolis known as Franklin, Indiana. Like any child new to a situation, the only thing my brother and I wanted to do was fit in—or at least not stick out. For us, this meant quickly trying to lose any trace of an accent. A minor chipping away of who I was in order to get along.

After a couple of years, we moved to Indianapolis. It wasn't too long before I was chosen for the Indianapolis Public School's budding Accelerated Program. This was the early 1980s. Apparently the unwritten rule of the Accelerated Program was that only two black students were allowed in at a time: one male, one female. And the way the program was set up, our class moved as a cohort through the system; this meant my peer group was locked in.

At home, we moved into an all-white subdivision. The flight to the west and north suburbs of Indianapolis hadn't begun yet, but other than by our immediate neighbors, we weren't well received. But we were encouraged to do our best to fit in. None of this was really an issue for my mother: as a Jamaican, her identity, culture, and history were so set and such a source of pride that she could have been dropped on Mars and she'd walk about like she owned the place.

It was otherwise for the rest of the family.

My parents weren't especially religious, but they wanted us to attend church. So they sent us with the neighbors across the way who worshiped at a small, fundamentalist, and all-white congregation.

To sum up, my neighborhood, school, and church life, the majority of my childhood and formative years, was set in an all-white environment.

My self-defined world was "colorless." I wanted to fit in and didn't want to acknowledge or play into my role as the Outsider. The Other. Instead, I inhabited a "colorblind" space. When my classmates spoke of black people, they "didn't mean me." I was no different from them: I spoke the same, listened to the same music, dressed in the same clothes, laughed at the same jokes. I was so absorbed into my peer culture—my (self-)hate so internalized—that I thought of other blacks as "them," even experiencing unease around them. Racism was an intellectual exercise, a social injustice to be stood against in theory, just nothing I experienced or chose to see.

Being colorblind worked because my blackness had been negated. I had a hole in me I didn't realize I had. I had always been "the weirdo" who retreated to the world of books. On the days when I wasn't busy not seeing myself as black (ignoring the jeers of "Oreo"), I saw myself as an emissary. Black people couldn't be all bad: "See? I'm not that different from you."

In 1989, my world was rocked by the movie *Do the Right Thing*. This demonstrates once again the eternal power of story. The day in the life of a black neighborhood, the racism the film's characters experienced, the anger, the tragedy hit me with such force that ten minutes after the credits rolled I remained in my seat. *Do the Right Thing* challenged—and by "challenged" I mean "shattered"—my world view. Suddenly, I saw the world through a racial lens.

Now everything in my world *had* to be black. I ate at black-owned restaurants, shopped at black-owned businesses. Watched black movies. Listened to black music, the more militant (Public Enemy, Poor Righteous Teachers, X-Clan) the better. I took Black Studies classes. And I was angry. Here's a sample from my journal at that time:

"Ours was a race that built great empires, civilizations, and culture. The only race to wander and conquer (in order to spread its self-declared superiority) is the white race. With slavery, they cut us off from our religion, culture, and language until we were the only race to have absolutely no identity. We couldn't even keep our true family names. A collective tabula rasa upon which the white man imprinted history, his language, his culture and sense of aesthetic and his religion. Why are we so integration crazed?

"We were brainwashed into thinking white is good, black is bad.... We were taught to think that the lighter your skin color is, the better you are....We were dubbed 'the Negro' and taught that our native Africa was peopled by heathen savages. We were raped, beaten, enslaved, worked, and tortured....

"We were taught to submit to and obey the white man by worshiping his alien (to us) white God (it's amazing how God and Jesus are always depicted as white).... Jesus spread his message in a meek and humble way. White people always spread his message with bloodshed."

It was also during this time that I began pursuing writing in a serious way. My first short story, "Soul Food" (published in *Hoodz*, 1999), was written during this time. It centered around that iconic black neighborhood institution, the barbershop, and told the tale of a sin-eater transformed into a figure of urban lore. My second story, "Family Business" (*Weird Tales* #338, 2006), explored a man returning to the Jamaican culture of his mother and plunging into a world he didn't understand.

The anger eventually ebbed as I tried to balance my "blackness" with the other worlds in which I operated. The anger and immersion of the previous phases were an over-reaction—the pendulum swinging so far in one direction to compensate for where I had started. Now, the pendulum was coming back to the middle; I, however, was trying to figure out where that middle was for me. I was defining what blackness meant to me, how I could carry my self-image and define my identity. Here, blackness takes on the dimension of praxis, theory accompanied by social action.

I began writing my first novel, "Strange Fruit" (still unpublished). It was the story of an interracial couple who return to their hometown in southern Indiana. The town was haunted by metaphoric and literal ghosts of its racist past. The novel follows the main character's journey of blackness/self-discovery as he figures out what being black in modern America means and how he's going to live in light of that meaning.

> *What is needed is not integration but a sense of worth*
> *in being black, and only black people can teach that.*
> *Black consciousness is the key to the Black man's eman-*
> *cipation from his distorted self-image.* —James Cone

For the longest time, blackness was a state of non-being. People ask why black people make such a big deal of black icons, black power mottos, question the high esteem in which Malcolm X is held. "Blackness" is a big deal because it is about reclaiming pride. Eschewing self-hatred. Being black means being true to who you are. Black self-consciousness and black experience encompass the totality of life and ideology, transcend individuality in the name of communal survival. So you know who you are, you're secure in what you are. Where does that leave me? I'm still not sure if I'm comfortable with this idea of blackness, if I want to carry this burden of race society feels so intent to foist on me. Race is an idea, not a fact.

The thing is, it seems like I'm only now at a place to begin to relate to others within my community and without. However history stands in my way, as if I have to traverse a long winding path of past hurts and grievances before I can deal or be dealt with by other people and groups as equals. Ultimately, I write as the Outsider—even within the black community, since I often feel a lack of place or connection or "right" to be there, I take on the role of the "invited guest." Writing has helped me explore this, too. In my novella, *Devil's Marionette* (Shroud Books, 2009) I wrestled with the role of the black artist: his responsibility to his craft and to the community.

One of the advantages to being "the other" is that often my perspective is that of an outsider. This is fine. I see outsiderness as a universal: everyone has felt like an outsider at one point or another. However, I have noticed that when I write stories with exclusively black characters I often get this feedback: "I felt like I was being preached at." Though I admit to a tendency toward preachiness. I think this feeling also stems from how race is perceived, especially how it's seen in terms of identity politics. White people, for example, don't have to think about race. It's the luxury of the majority, the luxury of privilege, to not have to worry about how race plays into the equation of life. In a black worldview, most things are defined by race. So black characters talking about racism to one another, though germaine to the story, might come across as preachy to a white reader. Yes, these are horrible over-generalizations, but my point is that being "forced" to confront an idea/reality you're not comfortable with can feel like being preached at.

Granted, writing as the other has led to some interesting reversals in my writing. Since I am a black writer and I write black characters a lot of the time, I've been playing with the idea of assuming the posture of the majority (this is more an intellectual exercise than anything else). In the stories I read, white characters don't announce their whiteness or make note that they were talking to other white characters. Yet, when an other enters the scene, race is automatically ascribed. I have noticed a tendency to "announce" the race of my characters in my own stories, a tendency that has never come up when my fellow black horror writers were discussing writing. So, assuming the posture of the majority, maybe I should only announce the race of a character when a white person enters the scene?

Most recently, the thoughts that have been dominating my writing have to do with where we blacks are as a people and where we could be. Where we are has been one of the predominant themes of my trilogy, Knights of Breton Court, beginning with *King Maker* (Angry Robot Books, 2010). I was at a pastor's convention a few years ago, and a pastor made a comment that stuck with me. He wondered aloud about whether the Israelites wandered the desert for 40 years, once Pharaoh released them, in order to get rid of the slave mentality. The Israelites had been enslaved for generations, and the culture of oppression became ingrained in their very scarred souls. It insinuated itself as part and parcel of their identity. So if in 1965 black people were "set free" as far as our civil rights, have we been wandering since then to get the "back of the bus" mentality out of our souls?

The ghetto mentality far too often defines "real" blackness. We devalue education in lieu of a quick ticket to the trappings of wealth. We esteem prison life and values. We devalue women, sex, and relationships (as if having babies made us men; or women, for that matter). Judging by many of our music videos (and too many television shows) we're still cooning for massa's amusement (the thought which actually inspired *Devil's Marionette*). The ghetto has become something to strive for in order to maintain realness rather than a place to get out off. Individualism, this "me first" narcissism which fragments community, is only one modern American value that we blacks as a people have bought into. Another is a rampant materialism that shrivels people's souls and empties their lives. Gold chains are still chains.

I don't want to be one of these middle-class brothers who either sits in judgment of the poor, or worse, forgets them because, "I've got mine." I have a lot of questions and too few answers. But my heart aches, aches in ways that are beyond words, when I see the loss of hope in the eyes of our young blacks. I get frustrated. I get angry. I write. The Knights of Breton Court was born from this. Taking a major figure from English lore, King Arthur, and re-imagining him in a new setting: the kingdom that was the end fruits of colonialism. The legacy of the inner city, with issues of homelessness, drugs, and gangs.

Our story, the story of black people in America—my story—is shaped by "white"-ness and white people. Our history is one of striving for legitimacy in "their" eyes via "their" ways. We constantly look at ourselves through the eyes of others. We engage in a brand of racial apologetics: defining blackness against white ideology and cultural aesthetics; a battle of superiority and legitimacy; racial life as a series of binary determinants. Thus we all become trapped in this endless cycle of trying to create criteria to define those in and out of any given group. And yet we can miss the point of these identifying stories and fail to see that our stories are actually quite similar.

Every people has a story to tell. When all is said and done, "blackness" (any racial identity) is about shared story. A story that defines us and continues to form us. When stories are reduced to law or dogma, their vitality is drained. When people no longer tell or listen to others' stories, they become locked in their provincial mindset, cultural ghettos of their own making. In fact, when people become totally removed from another's story, they become compelled to destroy those (others') stories, for they suggest other ways of living. Their stories become a threat.

My racial identity continues to inform much of my writing. It does this every bit as much as my faith does. I am a black, Christian man. That's my worldview, the lens through which I interpret reality. What does that mean for me in terms of race? I hear a lot of how "being black" is about "keeping it real," so I guess it all comes down to what "being real" actually means. Being real doesn't mean clinging to some sort of ghetto aesthetic and value system. Allow me to say that me "acting hood" would make me a minstrel, not "real," because that's not close to who I am or what I'm about. No, it boils down to personal authenticity and pride. What we can't afford to do is let one story keep us from participating in other stories. Maybe through the sharing of stories, the work of racial reconciliation can begin. I know it's the ultimate hope of my writing.

James H. Cone quote from *A Black Theology of Liberation*, Orbis Books, Maryknoll, NY, 1986.

Partial Transcript

by Terry Bisson

Due to technical difficulties, portions of this WisCon panel discussion were lost. We present what's left, unedited, for posterity: which is us, for in keeping with a literary gathering dedicated to the Fantastic, all the panelists were dead, in contrast with panels at other conventions where only every other participant is deceased.

The panelists were, in gender-corrected alphabetical order, Octavia E. Butler, James Baldwin, Emily Dickinson, Samuel Clemens, and Zora Neale Hurston. Salman Rushdie, a no-show, blamed an ineffective *fatwa*. There was no designated moderator: the dead abjure moderation. It is among their advantages.

Due to an unscheduled fistfight in the hallway, the designated recorder, Ms N. Ebullienfuss, arrived after the discussion was underway.

Clemens: ...never bothered with such nonsense in my day. A writer was a writer, and that was all.

Butler: Was a man, you mean. Assumed.

Hurston: A white man. Lily white. White as the driven snow. Blacks need not apply.

Baldwin: A straight white man, to be exact.

Clemens: Pish. No one knew. Or cared. Wasn't an issue.

Hurston: Of course not. It only becomes an issue when the outsider wants in. Then it becomes a struggle. The writer of color has to fight for what the white writer is given.

Butler: Or strive, at least.

Clemens: Isn't strive what we all do? Color, as you call it, can be an advantage. You stand out. Every writer wants to stand out. I wore white suits.

Baldwin: Loved that moustache, Sam. You and Buffalo Bill.

Butler. It's a restriction as well. It puts you in a box. You are expected to speak for the Race. You are caparisoned with expectations.

Dickinson: There's a hard rhyme.

Baldwin: The white writer, on the other hand, because he is still the default writer, is assumed to be speaking for the human race. Universality is a freebie. He's thought to have no axe to grind.

Clemens: I thought this panel was about you guys. Why is it focusing on me?

Baldwin: You see? The white writer is not a "racial" writer. He assumes any Race and Writing panel must be about us and not about him.

Hurston: His ethnicity is invisible, like water to a goldfish. He can put it on or take it off at will. Even if he is Jewish or regional, it is assumed he is talking about "larger matters." Take Faulkner....

Clemens: Faulkner was Jewish?

Dickinson: Is that a cigar?

Clemens: Only the best. Would you like one?

A section of the recording is lost due to shouting in the hall.

Butler: ...first thing a reader needs to know about a character after her gender? Unspecified, it's white.

Hurston: So we get Nigger Jim but not Cracker Huck.

Baldwin: And it's assumed if we introduce a Black character we are writing about Race.

Hurston: Sometimes we are.

Clemens: Of course. This is America. Hell, I wrote about race. It was the subtext of everything American in my day, the blackboard on which the social drama was written.

Hurston: In white chalk for the most part.

Butler: It still is today. But it's always assumed that we write about Race for more personal reasons.

Dickinson: Is that so bad?

Baldwin: It can be a diminishment. I like to think we write for the same reasons as every other damned scribbler: to play God.

Clemens: Bingo. Try one of these. You needn't inhale.

Thirty seconds of dialogue are lost due to the clashing of swords in the hallway.

Baldwin: Enough about literature. Let's talk about science fiction. An outsider venue. More inclusive, perhaps.

Hurston: Friendlier, for sure. An easier gate to crash.

Butler: True. But I wasn't forced into SF. The fact is, I always saw SF as a more serious, more expansive literature. It was a better fit than the so-called mainstream, which I always saw as a tributary with delusions of grandeur.

Clemens: I like this river talk. I did a little SF myself, but I never got a Big Mac.

Hurston: Just a ham sandwich!

Butler: No complaints here. But think about it: *Black female SF writer wins MacArthur.* When Jonathan Lethem won, it wasn't "White guy wins big prize." It was a bit of a diminishment. Too many modifiers.

Hurston: I like modifiers. Maybe you're being too sensitive.

Butler: I would claim that privilege too and not have it laid to race or gender.

Baldwin: The bane of the outsider.

Clemens: Outsiders! Aren't we all outsiders? Doesn't every writer wear that handy mask?

Hurston: Not all of us. Look at Jane Austen in that snug little circle of English gentry; she was no outsider.

Butler: Look again. A too-clever unmarried girl? I always identified with her outsiderness.

Dickinson: Hear hear, here.

Baldwin: Would someone please ask her to put that thing out?

Hurston: I'm not about to mess with her.

Clemens: So you are saying every writer is a racial writer, it's just that you are the only ones who know it.

Hurston: Right on. It's a gift, dude. A goldfish who knows she's a goldfish gains a certain perspective. Maybe that's why white writers never do so well with nonwhite characters. Nothing personal, but here comes Nigger Jim again.

Baldwin: Along with Queequeg.

Butler: Foils. Or maniacs. Look at Styron's Nat Turner.

Hurston: On the other hand, who can do white Italians as well as Spike Lee?

Clemens: 'Scuse me: Coppola?

Hurston: There you have it! Coppola does them as they imagine themselves to be. Spike Lee as they are.

Dickinson: Who's Spike Lee?

Baldwin: Hey, I thought we were talking about books, not movies.

Butler: Apparently you've never been on an SF convention panel before. We always end up talking about movies.

Hurston: We can't get books in Heaven anyway, just cable.

Baldwin: Heaven? I thought we were in Hell.

Clemens: Me too. Which reminds me….

At this point, the fight in the hall spilled over into the meeting room, and the rest of the dialogue is lost. Since it was a WisCon panel, it is assumed that all the points of contention were amiably resolved.

Racial Identity and Writing — Part Four

edited by Eileen Gunn

Do racial issues have more to do with what you write than those of social class or gender? Whichever way you answer, could you briefly explain why?

Yoon Ha Lee: At this point in time, yes. I don't spend a lot of time on class issues because I am not sure what I want to say about them yet. I don't do much with gender issues because it is frankly too painful to go there.

Nick Mamatas: No, I'd say that class has more to do with what I write than race, though trying to tease out how class is lived from race issues in the US, and thus in US settings, is nigh impossible.

Claire Light: No. Per my earlier response: that's what I live, that's what I see, that's how I think. Also: when you start to see and break down one social structure, all the rest come tumbling down.

Gavin Grant: I don't know. There are unconscious gender, class, and race structures that come through in my writing, and I try to make the stories not about those things. Even my own doppelganger—someone my own age and from my own background—would be a different universe, but I want to know more about life elsewhere. I read a critique of the most recent *Best American Short Stories* saying that it was full of the problems of rich people, which was cutting and seemed probable (haven't read the book yet). I liked when the editor of the Virginia Quarterly Review, Ted Genoways, put out a call for more gritty stories. He was panned for it online, but that seemed short-sighted to me: here's an editor asking for a type of stories taking on the harder parts of life (he was looking for stories not about rich people). Go write them!

Ben Rosenbaum: Well, not counting the whole Jewish thing, I feel like I am probably most sophisticated—in the sense that I tackled it earliest, started investigating it in conversations and seeing its effects in my life, and playing with it in fiction—about gender, followed perhaps by race? I feel most likely to put my foot in it about class, though I've been trying to address it more lately (e.g., in "The Guy Who Worked For Money").

Mark Rich: I am tempted to say social class. How to disentangle social attitudes from racial-cultural backgrounds, though? Strong social concerns likely spring from both Anglo-Swiss Mennonite/American Baptist influences and Japanese Shinto/Baptist influences.

Deb Taber: I tend to include more gender-issue themes than racial issues in my writing. In part, I think this is because gender as a social construct fascinates me. I never liked being thrust into gender-appropriate roles as a child, and I was raised to be "a person rather than a girl," to quote my mother. The real physical differences between the sexes, the societal roles that relate to gender, and the amazing gray area that is often ignored or maligned seem rich with stories to me. Racial differences are also rich, but so far they have not compelled me much as a writer. As a reader, I enjoy them very much.

Andrea Hairston: A character in a play I wrote in the early '80s, when asked to choose race, class, gender, sexuality loyalty/focus, said, "I am everything I am all the time." To write complex characters I have to consider the fullness of their lives. To create a complex world, I try to avoid saying a cow is a sphere—a great abstraction for certain measurements, for considering say, volume and mass—the legs are stubby and the head is beside the point—but this "spherical" cow is not what excites me about story telling. Focusing on gender or race or class without the rest leaves out too much of the story.

(Re)Producing the View from Nowhere: A Reaction to WisCon 34's Reproductive Health Panel

by Maria Velazquez

As I settled into my seat at the "Reproductive Health in Science Fiction and Fantasy" panel, I kept thinking of SuSu. SuSu was a Jelite prostitute in Nancy Kress's *An Alien Light*. She'd come to the fantastical city the Ged had created not because she wanted to win their fabulous technology for her people but because she was dying from whore's rot. There's a pivotal scene in *An Alien Light*, where she has barricaded herself in her room, away from the Jelite warriors intent on her sexual exploitation, realizing that she "do[es] not have to whore to eat" (84). Her refusal to be what her society requires women of her class background to be and the toll this takes on her sanity are part of what drives this novel forward. Her access to food, healthcare, and safety all impact her sexual and reproductive choices.

I read *An Alien Light* at a moment in my life when I was trying desperately to reconcile my education-access activist work—work that typically involves communities of color grappling with poverty and institutional racism—with my love for science fiction, a genre that often assumes a level playing field for its human characters. SuSu was my epiphany, the character whose fate in *An Alien Light* defined what it means for me to work towards utopia, and the character I kept thinking of during the "Activism: When To Speak Up, When to Let It Go" and "System Failure" panels. This was my first WisCon, and those two panels highlighted, for me, the stakes in imagining otherwise, the stakes in feminist science fiction and social justice work. The stakes are women like SuSu, women whose bodies have been judged public property, whose labor (reproductive and sexual) acts as the foundation of a society that is ultimately toxic.

In order to understand that moment in the text, where SuSu's access to food, health care, and a locked door spell safety and heightened agency, the reader has to know that SuSu grew up hungry, poor, and afraid. For SuSu, reproductive justice involves much more than access to a gynecologist; it involves an acknowledgement of her bodily sovereignty, and shifting social structures so that her "no" can mean "no." "If women do not have the right to choose what happens to our bodies, we risk relinquishing rights in all other areas of our lives" (hooks, 2000, p. 29,). Reproductive rights and access to reproductive healthcare are issues best examined using an intersectional lens, one that considers the matrix of domination framing everyday life. Basically this means you don't assume the biggest issue framing a woman's right to choose is whether or not she actually wants a baby. What options does she have? What options has she been presented with? The answers to both of these questions are contingent on her race, class, gender, region, sexuality, and access. "The meaning of our biological relationship to children is socially constructed in race, class, gender, and sexuality hierarchies and cannot be understood independent of these systems" (Weber, p. 84).

When I read *An Alien Light*, something clicked. Food, agency, safety: psychologist Abraham Maslow's triangle of needs as described in his 1943 book *A Theory of Human Motivation*. SuSu's life was consumed by a perpetual unsafety, an unsafety defined by her race, class, and gender. Her constant hunger and untreated STDs defined her; little did she realize how unwell she was until she had access to health care and food. Ian Hagemann's comment during the "System Failure" panel resonated with this. He said, "Safety is particularly important. Until I feel safe, I can't talk about my early childhood wounding." Until SuSu's most basic needs were met, those forming the first level of Maslow's pyramid, she could not begin addressing her psychological needs, those on Maslow's third level.

I hoped that this panel on reproductive health would engage with stories like this—stories about prostitutes, the poor, the forcibly sterilized, and the forgotten, people whose bodies become material fodder for politicized, classist, and militarized ideologies. I wanted to hear about SuSu and people like her, who negotiate with mysterious and unknown aliens in order to make their bodies safe. I wanted to hear about the Mary Choy's of the future—Choy is the titular heroine in Greg Bear's *Queen of Angels*, an Asian woman who's become a transform, who has used alien technology to make herself black and to give herself power over her fertility. I wanted to talk about Chloe, another of Bear's characters in that same series, whose husband "allows" her to give birth ex utero, even though his family is hugely politically and socially conservative. "What are your reproductive choices?" is not at all the same question as, "What reproductive choices are you allowed access to?" At its best, feminist science fiction explores both of these questions, challenging the reader to think further about those options they have taken for granted, and those technologies they have not yet been allowed access to. A conversation linking feminism, reproductive justice, and science fiction should engender the same kinds of epiphanies.

At the panel, we...didn't talk about any of those things, or anything like them. Janet Lafler began by saying that the closest thing we have to a uterine replicator is the incubator. I flinched—what about the bodies of Eastern European women and South Asian women, used as surrogates for women in the First World? The conversation moved on from there, with Gary Kloster insistently bringing up the all-male planet in Bujold's *Ethan of Athos*, the idea of replacing or eliminating the "need" for women (because really, all female bodies do is make babies), all with the underlying idea that this kind of technological evolution was all to the good. It was at this point that I realized that this was not a panel on reproductive justice. Also, I realized that the panelists were themselves deeply unprepared for leading this kind of discussion—which is one of the reasons this essay acts as a response and not a summary. How can you summarize a scattering of points whose main commonality is a tone of "Ooooooooh! Science fiction is cool!"? Instead, I am working to convey the gist of the panelists' commentary, and my emotional and intellectual engagement with it.

Asking the "What's at stake?" question endemic to social justice work would have clarified not just the parameters of the conversation, but also what bodies were under discussion, why, and by whom. This lack of clarification deeply impacted the way the panel was structured, because the panelists themselves often fell into the trap of defining reproductive health strictly in its relation to abortion and pregnancy. In

Feminism is for Everybody, bell hooks highlights that this conflation of reproductive health with the pro-choice movement is the purview of a feminism defined by activists in positions of class power. In her critique of the mass media's portrayal of reproductive rights issues, and the reductive nature of this brand of feminism's politics, hooks highlights that bodily sovereignty in the context of medicalized technologies is not something everybody can take for granted. She writes that "[l]ong range medical problems from cesareans and hysterectomies were not juicy subjects for mass media; they actually called attention to a capitalist patriarchal male-dominated medical system that controlled women's bodies and did with them anything they wanted to do" (hooks, 2000, p. 27).

A quick reading of tomes like *Unequal Treatment: Confronting Racial and Ethnic Disparities in Healthcare* or *Conquest: Sexual Violence and the American Indian Genocide* highlight what's at stake for women of color and poor women and their relationship to their healthcare providers: the ability to choose or not to choose to have children, to breastfeed, to have children at a later date, to receive medical treatment without being subject to verbal or sexual assault. Indeed, a quick viewing of *Miss Evers' Boys*, the film about the Tuskegee Study of Untreated Blacks with Syphilis, would have illustrated that the reproductive health issues facing men go far beyond their inability to have children without uterine replicators.

How can you have a sustained conversation about reproductive health *without mentioning* reproductive justice? As the panel progressed, I realized that the panelists were more interested in talking about the technological potential of a First World future than about reproductive health as it pertains to living bodies. The view from nowhere (a term some feminists, like Donna Haraway, use to mark out a viewpoint seen as being normative and neutral that is in actuality taking whiteness and privilege as its default) remained unchallenged. In fact, at one point a panelist described the application process in Anne McCaffrey's Pegasus series as neutral. How can you say that applying to have kids and having your genes judged is at all a neutral process? Particularly in a world where one of the main female characters, Tirla, is both an illegal, unapproved child and described as "ripen[ing] a lot faster than we Northern and Occidental types" (p. 446) because she's not white? McCaffrey is not describing a "neutral" system. While she's actively critiquing a welfare state that judges some of its citizens as unfit to breed, at the same time she's supporting a raced and classed discourse that locates some women's bodies as hyper-fertile.

I am not exaggerating when I say I was vibrating with anger. Not only were the panelists being dismissive of historical context (for example, using Huxley's *Brave New World* as an example of a reproductive dystopia, without mentioning that Huxley was a huge eugenicist), it was also unclear that they'd researched their topics, or had any sense of the history of the terms they were calling on. Reproductive health, for example, calls up the ghosts of specific histories of resistance in womanist, feminist, and anti-racist movements.

Access, another concept referred to during the panel, isn't about convenience. It's about safety, materiality, and the social structures that keep bodies in place and unsafe. Earlier this year, UnusualMusic of the blog *Angry Black Woman* posted an extensive history of reproductive justice in the US, highlighting its history in communities of color and its holistic underpinnings. UnusualMusic quotes SisterSong, a reproductive rights organization, who says: "Abortion isolated from other social justice/human rights issues neglects issues of economic justice, the environment, immigrants' rights, disability rights, discrimination based on race and sexual orientation, and a host of other community-centered concerns directly affecting an individual woman's decision-making process" (UnusualMusic, 2010). The organizations to which UnusualMusic linked consistently emphasized that access to reproductive healthcare is intimately tied to multiple types of identities. That the panelists would not work to situate a panel on reproductive health in a way that reflected the ongoing conversations about these issues in the black feminist blogosphere is more than simply careless; it reflects a kind of dismissive entitlement that insists the only bodies worth describing are those bodies with class- and race-based privilege.

Unfortunately, this dismissive entitlement reflects larger issues in the feminist movement as a whole. Even *MS Magazine*, which normally is very conscious about representing the voices of all its readers, featured a celebration of the pill that left out its origin story, particularly its testing on Puerto Rican women. This testing was performed without the informed consent of these women, women who were penalized for being Latina, working class, and undereducated by becoming guinea pigs for a major pharmaceutical company (as depicted in the PBS film *The Puerto Rico Pill Trials*).

Lisa Wade, a blogger with *Sociological Images*, highlights how conventional conversations about reproductive rights often center on choosing or not choosing a particular form of birth control. She describes the lack of options presented to women of color and poor women, paying particular attention to the refusal of some doctors to offer their patients a variety of options and to the conflation of reproductive choice with the state through the welfare system and the state's interest in policing the size of "unfit" families. In *Understanding Race, Class, and Gender*, Weber writes that "[t]he rights of some women to be mothers depends, in fact, on the lack of rights among other women to retain their status as mothers, highlighting the boom in the international adoption of white babies after white, middle-class women in the US had access to abortion" (Weber, p. 83). Weber argues that white women's ability to choose to not produce white babies depended in many ways on the inability of other women to choose to keep their babies globally, emphasizing that in this present system rights, access, and impact are not distributed evenly.

Next we began talking about STIs and STDs, referring to books like Peter S. Beagle's *Lila the Werewolf* and Scott Westerfeld's *Peeps*, where the specter of disease has a mystical component. Great. Because all those real-life diseases are cured and now only need symbolic cognates, am I right? Some audience members also brought up *Clay's Ark, The Immortal Life of Henrietta Lacks*, and *Wild Seed*. Not once did the panelists engage in a sustained conversation about bodily sovereignty as it manifests in one's ownership of one's DNA; forced pregnancies; or a sustained discussion of consent, the state, or the corporation in terms of maintaining bodily sovereignty; or the way one's positioning in regards to access to reproductive health care is dependent one's identities.

At this point, my notes descended into rage. Honestly, they were pretty rage-y throughout this panel, since I felt like I'd fallen into a Twilight Zone of well-intentioned privilege. There was little discussion of infertility and aging, little discussion of consent except as a given, and little troubling of the idea that medical encroachments onto someone's body would be anything but desirable. At the panel's end I left the room furious and disappointed.

As I was leaving, another audience member followed me to ask about one of the sources I'd mentioned, *Operation Bootstrap*, a documentary about the relationship between US industrialization of Puerto Rico and the sterilization of Puerto Rican women. I gave her the citation, a little stunned that someone in the audience had thought I'd said something useful, since I'd felt so angry. I then staggered down to the Safer Space for People of Color, and vented about what I'd wanted—needed—that panel to be. This was actually an amazing moment for me politically— immediately, Nora K. Jemisin, who is totally amazing, and Jessica Kaiser, a panelist from "System Failure," listened to my account of the issues that I saw in the panel and helped me to articulate what I perceived as major items of concern. My notes from that conversation represent the earliest draft of this essay. Without their patient brainstorming, this discussion of privilege, social justice, and writing would not exist.

There is something wrong with a panel on reproductive health that centers itself on technologies instead of on bodies. More importantly, there's something wrong with a panel that seems to assume that because it's "not another fucking race panel" that there is no need to talk about race. Or class. Or gender. Or how silencing it is to assume political neutrality, structural access, and common cultural histories in conversations about possessing bodily sovereignty. Or what a contextual privilege it is to be able to choose.

Bibliography

Haraway, D. (1988). Situated Knowledges. *Feminist Studies, 14*(3), 575-599.

hooks, b. (2000). *Feminism is for Everybody.* Cambridge, MA: South End Press.

Kress, N. (1987). *An Alien Light.* New York: Arbor House.

May, E. T. (2010, Spring). *The Pill Turns 50.* Retrieved August 17, 2010, from MS Magazine: http://www.msmagazine.com/spring2010/thepill.asp

McCaffrey, A. (1990). Pegasus In Flight. In A. McCaffrey, *The Wings of Pegasus* (pp. 209-446). New York: Guild America Books.

The Puerto Rico Pill Trials. (n.d.). Retrieved January 10, 2011, from PBS: http://www.pbs.org/wgbh/amex/pill/peopleevents/e_puertorico.html

UnusualMusic. (2010, February 26). *Reproductive Justice Linkspam: A Starting Point.* Retrieved July 28, 2010, from Angry Black Woman: http://theangryblackwoman.com/2010/02/26/reproductive-justice-linkspam-a-starting-point/

Wade, L. (2010, June 10). *Breaking Down the Force/Choice Binary in the Sterilization of Women of Color.* Retrieved August 17, 2010, from Sociological Images: http://thesocietypages.org/socimages/2010/06/21/ breaking-down-the-forcechoice-binary-in-the-sterilization-of-women-of-color/

Weber, L. (2001). *Understanding Race Class Gender and Sexuality: A Conceptual Framework.* New York: McGraw-Hill.

Biting Tongues

(for WisCon)
by Amal El-Mohtar

Speak to us in silk, they say,
speak to us in milk,
be pillow-soft, be satin-smooth,
be home-spun sugar sweet.

We part our lips. We breathe our breaths.
We bite our tongues and swallow blood
knot stones into our stomachs, heave
and spit red salt where words should be,
stitch shut our mouths with stubborn thread
to spare our tablecloths.

Such a mess! If you can't say something nice,
if you can't be honey cinnamon spice
if you can't be dusky-eyed candy mice
shut the fuck up, you stuck-up bitch
you whore you cunt you slag you witch
where you going dressed like that
red as meat and us so hungry?
What did you think would happen, huh?
What did you think would happen?

We are told
of wolves in the world, and we but girls.
We are told
of girls in the world, and they but wolves
who cannot help themselves.
We are told
to be girls or wolves,
be eaten or hungry,

but we are never hungry
who make meals of ourselves,
who chew the insides of our cheeks,
bleed into our bellies.
We are told
that to be bold is to be bled,
that red's what brings the wolves around,
that we're better off drowned.

They come with axes,
cut us to pull the good girls out.

They leave us with our bloodstone bellies,
our sewn up mouths, our halted breaths,
and a river for a bed.

Until one of us
with sharpest teeth
and shredded mouth
rips silence from our lips
with a battle-cry kiss, and says

we speak as we are
with tongues of snake and hummingbird
of ocean and of earth
of sky and salt and smoke and fire
of gesture, ink, and ringing bells.

We speak as we are
with bodies various as motion
voices of muscle and music and colour
beautiful bloody mouths.

We paint with tumblebroken words
we sing loud with our speaking hands
unmake the bodies shaped for us
and lip to eye to fingertip
we spill our red-mouth stories out
and listen, taste them on the air
with our forked and biting tongues.

Song for an Ancient City

by Amal El-Mohtar

Merchant, keep your attar of roses,
your ambers, your oud,
your myrrh and sandalwood. I need
nothing but this dust
palmed in my hand's cup
like a coin, like a mustard seed,
like a rusted key.
I need
no more than this, this earth
that isn't earth, but breath,
the exhalation of a living city, the song
of a flute-boned woman,
air and marrow on her lips. This dust,
shaken from a drum, a door opening, a girl's heel
on stone steps, this dust
like powdered cinnamon, I would wear
as other girls wear jasmine and lilies,
that a child with seafoam eyes
and dusky skin might cry, *there*
goes a girl with seven thousand years
at the hollow of her throat, there
goes a girl who opens her mouth to pour
caravans, mamelukes, a Mongolian horde
from lips that know less of roses
than of temples in the rising sun!

Damascus, Dimashq
is a song I sing to myself. I would find
where she keeps her mouth, meet it with mine,
press my hand against her palm
and see if our fingers match. She
is the sound, the feel
of coins shaken in a cup, of dice,
the alabaster clap of knight claiming rook,
of kings castling—she is the clamour
of tambourines and dirbakki,
nays sighing, qanouns musing, the complaint
of you merchants with spice-lined hands,
and there is dust in her laughter.

I would drink it, dry my tongue
with this noise, these narrow streets,
until she is a parched pain in my throat, a thorned rose
growing outwards from my belly's pit, aching fragrance
into my lungs. I need no other. I
would spill attar from my eyes,
mix her dust with my salt,
steep my fingers in her stone
and raise them to my lips.

أغنية إلى مدينة قديمة:

الشاعرة: أمال المهتار

ترجمة: أسامة عجاج المهتار

بريشة عصام درويش

دعني من عطرك يا عطار
دعني من وردك والعنبر
من عطر العود، من المُر
دعني من خشب الصندل
دعني من عطرك يا عطار

كل ما أحتاجه بعضُ غبارُ
أضمه في راحتي الصغيرة
كقطعة نقد، كحبة خردلٍ
كمفتاح وشمه الصدأ
كل ما أحتاجه هذه الأرض
التي ليست بأرض
بل زفير مدينة تنبض بالحياة
أغنية امرأة عظامها نايات
تلعب فيها الريح
ويرقص الهواء على شفتين تقطران نسغاً يفيض
بالحياة

هذا الغبار المهتزُّ من قرع الطبول
المتساقط من فتحة باب، من دعسة بنت حافية
فوق الأدراج الحجرية
هذا الغبار بلون القرفة ألبسه عطراً كما الصبايا
يلبس عطر الياسمين والليلك
فتشير فتاة عيناها من زيد البحر
وجلدها بلون الغسق صارخة:
ها صبيّة في فجوة حنجرتها سبعة آلاف سنة،
ها صبيّة تصب من فمها القوافل والمماليك
ومن شفتين تعرفان عن معابد الشمس
أكثر من الورد، تزحف جحافل المغول.

داماس، دمشق، أغنية أنشدها لنفسي
أبحث عن فمها ليلتقي بفمي
أجمع راحة يدي إلى راحة يدها
أتأمل تطابق الأصابع

إنها ملمس النقود المعدنية ورنّتها إذ تهتزُ
في فنجان نحاسي
إنها النردُ، تبييت الملك في لعبة شطرنج
طعق الخيال على المرمر إذ يجتاح البرج

هي صخب الدفوف والدريكة
تنهيدة الناي وتأمل القانون
إنها شكواكم يا عطار، شكوى أيادي التجار
المصبوغة بألوان التوابل
أما ضحكتها فيشوبها الغبار يا عطار
أودّ لو أشرب هذا الغبار
ينشّف فمي هذا الضجيج
هذه الأزقة
تصبح ألماً صحراوياً في حنجرتي
وردة شوكية تخرج من أحشائي
عطراً موجعاً في رئتي لا أتعطر بغيره.

سأسكب العطر من عيني يا عطار
أخلط ملحه بغبارها
أحمّر أناملي في حجارتها
وأرفعها إلى شفتي.

Translated into Arabic by Oussama Ajaj El-Mohtar and illustrated by Issam Darwish

ترجمة قصيدة Song to an Ancient City التي حلّت
في المرتبة الأولى في Rhysling Award للشعر التأمّلي
2009. والتي تنظّمها مؤسسة Science Fiction Poetry
Association في أميركا سنوياً.
القصيدة لأمال المهتار، شاعرة كندية من أصل لبناني. وطالبة
دكتوراه في الأدب الإنكليزي في جامعة Exeter، في المملكة
المتحدة.

The Meaning of this Translation

by Amal El-Mohtar

Last summer, my father and I were sitting at the kitchen table together, both tapping away at our laptops, to the amusement of my mother and sister. Every now and then, my father would pause to ask me a question.

The questions were slightly odd—even slightly mysterious. "How would you say this?" he'd ask. "What does this word mean, in this context?" It quickly became apparent that he was asking me about words and phrases in my poem "Song for an Ancient City," the one I presented at WisCon 34 during the "Split Tongues" reading. But to what end he asked these questions wasn't completely clear.

A few minutes later, he read "Song for an Ancient City" to me in Arabic.

Let me explain the significance of this. I was born in Canada, and Arabic was my first language; my parents speak with sad fondness of how easily I used to natter at people in it, how sweet it was to hear me say all my "ees" as "ums." It was my first language, the language in which I spoke my first words, the only language I knew for at least a few years of my life.

But I can't remember ever thinking in Arabic.

I spoke and speak it, yes, can read and write it very basically, but even when we lived in Lebanon for two years when I was little, even when I went to schools taught and administered in Arabic, English was the language of my mind, the language in which I read books, the language I felt most comfortable speaking. I felt put upon when my parents insisted I speak to them in Arabic; I felt stifled. Once we were back in Canada, when I was about nine, I detested being forced to go to Arabic school on Saturdays, detested being forced to trot out stilted syllables in company, to embarrass myself, when I felt I could communicate so eloquently in English. I spoke French more fluently. I resented being ex-pected to speak Arabic, and resented my parents telling me how sorry I would be, in a few years, when I understood what I was missing.

They told me how annoyed I would be not to understand a joke that had just been spoken in Arabic; sometimes they put my loss in terms of mild competition, knowing how competitive I was, saying, "Listen to how beautifully so-and-so's children speak," or "Don't you wish you could read this book?" I don't know if they knew, then, how much I would come to understand about what I'm missing—literally, what is missing from me.

What is missing from me are stories and folktales told to me in Arabic. What is missing from me are the songs my mother's mother would sing, make up on the spot just for us, that I remember nothing of but her voice. What is missing from me is the poetry of my father's father, which I only know in English approximations told to me by my parents. What is missing from me is the certainty that my children will grow up speaking Arabic, because if my parents couldn't give me all their fluency, how could my fifth-grade comprehension hope to raise a mind able to think in anything but English?

What is missing from me is the ability to write "Song for an Ancient City" in Arabic.

To hear my father read it to me was to feel that he was showing me, in my own words, what was missing from me—but also that he held it there, was keeping it for me, that it wasn't lost but misplaced, that I could find it if I wandered Damascus long enough, looking for it. To hear him choke up while reading it was to be unable to keep from crying my-self, to hear what that poem ought to have been, how much more it was in the language of the city I was attempting to describe.

But at the same time, I know that I couldn't have written it in Arabic, not quite that way. During RaceFail09, Deepa D wrote about how she didn't dream of dragons; she also spoke of language and how she felt she had "half a tongue." That struck me most of anything she said. Ultimately it led to Shweta Narayan and me deciding to build a reading around that theme and call it "Split Tongues" to foreground the often troubled re-lationship we felt we had with the language of our thoughts.[1] This is a piece of what I said to Deepa D in my online reply:

"I think there's also a benefit to having half a tongue: you're able to write things like this for an English-speaking audience. You're able to bridge a huge gap with that other half. I feel that my English fluency gives me this responsibility to mediate, to educate, and I'm aware that in my community, the ability to communicate, to articulate, is an incredible blessing."

So I'm aware of this, and it helps balance the pain of feeling I've failed my first language, my culture, by being lazy, by being shortsighted. It makes me more keen than ever to remedy it, to spend enough time in Syria and Lebanon to build something beautiful on the foundations I have. It makes me realize that perhaps I couldn't have written "Song for an Ancient City" without that hole where language should be, aching to be filled. It makes me want to write more.

Endnote

1. Shweta's poem "Nagapadam," which I read on her behalf at "Split Tongues," addresses this explicitly. You can find it online in the first issue of *Stone Telling* (http://stonetelling.com/index.html), a magazine of boundary-crossing poetry, which takes diversity as its mandate.

You Are Not Alone: Fighting Impostor Syndrome

by Heidi Waterhouse and Jess Adams

Panel description: Fighting Impostor Syndrome

Do you ever feel like you are not nearly as smart/cool/together/awesome as other people seem to think you are? Do you feel like you are constantly faking competence and that at any second you will be revealed as a fraud? Do you wonder why other women do not seem as plagued by this problem as you are? Most of us are. Published authors, awesome bloggers, amazing mothers, fierce feminists—many of us are in the same boat. Let's get together and talk about how we work through those feelings, why we have them, and how we can avoid passing them on to the next generation of women.

Panelists: Heidi Waterhouse (M), Jess Adams, Nick Murphy, Jennifer Pelland, Lynne M. Thomas

Why this panel, why these people

Heidi: This is the panel I worried about most. I am amused by the irony.

Jess: My notes start with the following: "I'm on a stage...." I definitely had the momentary sensation of not belonging on a stage! When I first got my panel assignment, I was like, "I can't sit this panel. There's no way I can talk intelligently about Impostor Syndrome!" Which, of course, is the Impostor Syndrome talking.

Heidi: I proposed this panel because I felt passionately that it changed my life when someone explained the concept of

Impostor Syndrome to me, and I wanted to share that with other people, and a WisCon panel seemed like the best way. When I proposed it, I imagined perhaps twelve people sitting in a circle and sharing their experiences. I kept up this fond belief until Joanna wrote to ask me how I felt about being in one of the ballrooms. I had to drastically rethink how many people wanted to hear about this concept. The more people there were in the audience, the more anxious I got that someone in the audience would know more than I did on the subject.

This is the crux of the problem, of course. My fears tell me that the more people who see me as confident, the easier it is to find the one doubter who will turn the whole crowd, and everyone will realize that there is someone small and fallible behind the wizard's curtain.

We settled in, introduced ourselves, and talked about our own manifestations of Impostor Syndrome. Nick had what he identified as "acute onset" Impostor Syndrome, meaning there was a watershed moment at which he was made to feel like an impostor. The rest of us seemed to feel that if we had accomplished something, it was obviously something trivial and should have been "better" in some way. It was fascinating to watch us all try not to apologize for who we were, or minimize ourselves. The published authors talked about feeling like it was a fluke that they got published, the academics talked about feeling like it was luck rather than skill that had gotten them through school. I think all of us struggled with feeling like it was our privilege or luck that gave us our current positions.

Jess: What was powerful to me was hearing other panelists who have already accomplished the things I sometimes berate myself for not accomplishing discuss their experiences. It was pretty eye-opening to realize that there's not some magic fix for feeling this way—simply accomplishing the thing(s) you think must be done doesn't automatically abolish Impostor Syndrome. My fellow panelists have written books, finished grad school, had successful careers in their chosen fields—these are all the things I'm down on myself for not having done yet. Of course, Impostor Syndrome is not just about accomplishing things in life; it's also largely about feeling as if you accomplished those things *in spite of* your personal inherent tendency to, you know, *suck.*

Why we doubt ourselves

Heidi: We talked about ways we were raised, and how high standards are both good and bad. For example, high expectations drove me to meet them, but if I couldn't completely meet them, I felt like a failure in all areas, not just the ones I had failed at.

We talked about the work of raising children and housekeeping, and I said, "What we do [in the home sphere] has value even if it doesn't have status." We talked about how much American culture equates money with worth. This is especially hard on the self-conception of people who do uncompensated work—parenting, housekeeping, even writing fanfic or maintaining online communities. We talked about how much we respect other people for their accomplishments while not doing a good job of respecting our own, similar accomplishments.

Jess: It seems that Impostor Syndrome often starts to take root with socialization that instructs us (either explicitly or implicitly) not to be prideful, not to boast, not to be conceited. Panelists spoke about the various ways these messages are delivered to us, such as gender socialization and cultural socialization. Some of us spoke about coming out of regional cultures where humility is highly valued. We also addressed how mental health issues can generate or exacerbate Impostor Syndrome, because they can make you doubt your own observations and self-worth.

The panel noted that there is a gendered/gender-socialized tendency for women to be more prone to Impostor Syndrome. In U.S. culture, women are often socialized to deflect praise or compliments, and to downplay achievements with language like, "Oh, it was nothing!" Often, activities traditionally thought of as "women's work" are brushed aside. There was some discussion about the difference between "value" and "status," and about how "women's work" is discounted regardless of the gender of the person performing that work.

We are not alone

Heidi: And then, oh best beloved, we had the audience participation part of the panel.

I had previously printed and handed out sheets of paper that had "You Are Not Alone" printed on the front in huge letters. I took the microphone down and stood in front of the dais and invited audience members to come up and give a description of something that made them feel like an impostor, or frightened them. If an audience member had a similar experience, they raised their sign or hands. This ended up working out better than I could ever have imagined. The member up front got to watch as waves of affirmation rolled across the audience. The audience got to look around and see the people next to them having similar experiences. I know that I fought really hard not to cry at the sheer connectedness of watching people get it, really get it, that they weren't the only people who had this problem, whatever it was.

I am going to paraphrase a few of the statements that I remember getting especially significant reactions. I wish, oh, I wish that I'd thought to record this somehow.

♦   I have gone to a lot of college, but I still don't know what I want to be when I grow up.

♦   I don't feel smart enough to be at WisCon.

♦   I'm not published/published enough to feel like a real author.

♦   I don't do enough work to be a real feminist.

- I work in academia, and I always feel outranked/outsmarted.

- I work in technology, and I feel lonely.

- I work at home, and I don't feel taken seriously.

- I had to sacrifice part of my career to support my family.

- I have a mental illness, and it makes me second-guess my interactions and perceptions.

It was amazing to watch the surprise and delight on people's faces as they realized that truly, they were not alone.

Jess: The value in hearing something as simple as *"You are not alone"* can't be overstated. At one point, you turned to me and said, "I think I might cry!" Yeah! I thought so, too! I can't recall any statement that didn't have at least one or two people who spoke up to say they'd experienced the same feeling. We ran the time out on the panel this way, and it was *awesome*.

What we learned

Jess: So much of my personal experience with Impostor Syndrome has been about that voice somewhere in my head telling me that this is just the way I am—on a basic level, I am not good enough, smart enough, accomplished enough. There was a real feeling that all of these other people succeed where I've failed. It was revelatory to hear perspectives from other people, to hear other people speak up and voice the same thoughts I've had. I notice that when I hear others saying these things, my response is, "No! *You're not a failure."* I am compassionate to other people in a way that is difficult for me to extend to myself. I think that this WisCon experience of hearing other people speak about their own circumstances, seeing and hearing that for every one there were people who felt "*Me, too,"* really helped me to start figuring out how to start changing this mindset.

Heidi: I think the panelists' takeaway was that it was really enlightening and empowering to find out that other people we respect may be feeling like they are also only pretending to be competent, but really we are pretty competent. Also that talking about and demystifying Impostor Syndrome serves other people who may not have encountered the theory.

Jess: At WisCon 34, I had the same experience over and over again, possibly because I had this panel on my mind and so I was primed to think about it and notice it. I had these moments of being in the middle of a sentence, with several people engaged and listening to me—and I realize that those people were some of the people I most respected and admired, and yet somehow they were talking to *me*. These little moments of cognitive dissonance were surprising because at the very moment my brain piped up to tell me *This can't be happening, they're about to figure you out,* I was realizing that this feeling is Impostor Syndrome in action.

What you can do about Impostor Syndrome

Talk about it. The next time a friend tells you that it's just luck she got that promotion, affirm that she deserved it and point out that there may be an external reason she feels this way.

Keep being competent yourself, and learn to accept compliments as your due, rather than something to be rejected gracefully.

If you find it difficult to genuinely accept a compliment, try simply saying, "Thank you." In other words, "Fake it 'til you make it." Sometimes it takes practice!

It may also help to think of accepting a compliment as doing a favor for the person who is complimenting you.

When you are offered constructive feedback, remind yourself that if someone is suggesting ways you might change or do something differently, they believe that you are capable enough to do so.

Remind yourself of the things you're good at. If necessary, take time to write a list of what you've accomplished and the ways you've demonstrated competency, or even awesomeness.

Keep in mind that fighting Impostor Syndrome is a process. You may always have that sense of self doubt, but coping with it is a skill that can be learned, just like any other skill.

Seek out others in your community or field, and work to build a support network. Remember, *You are not alone*! A group of peers who can help to reflect your own competencies will bolster you, and you will be able to help show them that they are not alone, either.

Racial Identity and Writing — Part Five

edited by Eileen Gunn

Do you think science fiction and fantasy are particularly well suited or ill suited for the examination of racial issues? Are there specific writers who have addressed racial issues in a way that was particularly meaningful to you (for good or bad — your call)? Did or does this influence your own writing? In what way?

Claire Light: Yes.

Octavia Butler, Nalo Hopkinson, Samuel R. Delany (I know it's the trifecta, but they were the first sf writers I read with any sort of intentionality.)

Yes. They make me want to do the sorts of things that they do and as well as they do them—to do for others what they did for me. The usual role model stuff.

Ben Rosenbaum: Sure, they are particularly well suited. Sf is all about otherness, transformation, and the long historical view, and is good at sneaking up on topics by removing them to distant venues.

Octavia Butler, for one, was a huge influence; and her bravery and her brilliant, playful, harsh imagination in re-imagining race is one example of why. (Consider, say, the awful complicities and mutual need and subtle mutual violence and power imbalance between alien species in "Bloodchild"...)

Gavin Grant: I think sf/f gives a space to explore possibilities in the way mimetic fiction (or whatever you want to call it) doesn't.

I love books that show me the present or futures that are logical but fresh, such as Nalo Hopkinson's *Midnight Robber,* Raphael Carter's *The Fortunate Fall,* Kim Stanley Robinson's Mars books, *Love & Rockets,* Octavia Butler's *Parable of the Sower* (and the Seed books), and Jon Courtenay Grimwood's Arabesk series. But James Sallis's Lew Griffin mysteries are proof that amazing racial/gender/class novels can be written in any genre.

Andrea Hairston: Octavia Butler inspired me with her complex characters and relentlessly challenging plots and no-win situations. What she did with gender, race, and class, with the world we might take for granted, really messed with my mind. I am still haunted by her stories and novels, many years after first reading. John Sayles' complex, multi-character films with interaction and story as their core also have inspired me. Their work validated my impulses.

Yoon Ha Lee: I'm not convinced sf/f are any better or worse at examining racial issues than other genres, but I haven't read a lot of fiction outside of sf/f so it's hard to say.

For an excellent treatment of racial issues, I really loved Colson Whitehead's *The Intuitionist.* For a bad example, I have to cite Raymond Feist and Janny Wurts' Empire trilogy, which featured, among other things, a more-or-less Asian protagonist being shown the evil of her cultural ways by a white man who Knew Better, I suppose, by virtue of being white. I was not charmed.

I suppose the bad examples are actually the ones that inspire me to try to handle this better, although I'm sure I have a long way to go.

Mark Rich: In American terms, both forms seem to have been particularly ill-suited, for a long time. The wonder stories of the 1860s through the earlier 1900s relied on a goodly amount of racism for their audience appeal. Similarly, race-inspired fears fed into fantasy stories ranging from the rapture novelists to the perhaps regrettably canonized H.P. Lovecraft, during the latter part of that time frame. As the wonder story became "science fiction," however, a progressive element began coming to the fore, thanks to the Jewish-intellectual writers of Manhattan and some U.K. writers, including Olaf Stapledon.

A few John Brunner novels come to mind, which I enjoyed, in which he presented race-related matters in ways that likely won over his readership more easily than would have been the case had he written them as contemporary-realistic. Brunner and others raised the field by using sf as a platform of this sort. Since then, however, sf has come to mean, for many people, a game-like pseudo-sf. By and large, it is no longer a symbolist form. Race issues are probably useful in these new works, as window-dressing. As to fantasy...the instinct toward fantasy in American writers produced such a bibliographic weight of literary intolerance that we should be surprised when any new American fantasists try to muscle the form up into respectability.

I for one am surprised, now that I think about it. And does my surprise tempt me to try? Hmmm....

Nick Mamatas: I'd say that sf and fantasy are particularly poorly suited for the examination of racial issues, except in the most jejune and retrograde of ways. That is, those mythical purple and green people from the old saw, "I don't care if someone is white, black, brown, yellow, or green or purple!" tend to be trotted onto stage with depressing regularity. Between writers who make their aliens essentially Asian in order to make them different from the "people" in their stories, to the Monster Manual-methodology of fantasy (you weren't using these gods and monsters, were you?) sf/f as a literary tradition is almost hopeless.

As an abstraction—the sort of writing in which one can literalize any metaphor and have one's work read by young people whose political and social opinions haven't yet been set and ossified—sf/f has great potential for exploring racial issues. In practice and as a matter of history though, it hasn't done this very much. Certainly not in the hardcore of either sf or fantasy; when it's been done (e.g., some elements of the New Wave, the parts of feminist sf that are racially aware) it's explicitly as a counter-hegemonic within the genre. That is, to best explore racial issues in sf/f, one has to set one's writing against sf/f as it is (re)produced by the publishing industry and most writers, and against the tacit demands of most genre readers.

I've also noticed a very specific and generally unremarked-upon tendency in fantasists to engage in casual antiziganism or to romanticize, exoticize, and appropriate Roma/Sinti culture. I find this especially disgusting because it is incredibly common, and many of the self-selected activists and allies within the community of sf/f writers don't even perceive it. Word to the wise: don't call yourself a "gypsy" if you ain't one.

Amal El-Mohtar: I think science fiction and fantasy are particularly well-suited to the examination of racial issues slantwise; I think our genres enable readers to engage with racial issues in a way that bypasses their own biases by placing those issues in an unfamiliar context. This has its disadvantages, of course: allegory can be clunky and unsophisticated, while especially subtle treatments might just whoosh over readers' heads in a way that leaves them clueless as to their relevance to reality.

Further, I think issues of race in fantasy and sf are also particularly vulnerable to dismissal. I think of all the times that people have responded to a shortcoming in the treatment of racial issues with something like "It's a DIFFERENT WORLD," or "It's the FUTURE, get OVER it," as if an author's writing isn't informed by the racial tensions and politics of *this* world, of our present moment.

It's sad, but the most meaningful treatments of race that spring to mind are the bad ones, the ones that made me furious. The first of these — possibly the first time I ever realized that writers were not holy creatures who could do no wrong, purely by virtue of their having written books — was C. S. Lewis' Chronicles of Narnia. I read them all through for the first time when I was sixteen, and by *The Horse and His Boy*, was getting decidedly growly at the fact that the good people-who-look-Arab-and-don't-worship-Aslan were exceptions to a general rule of violent malevolence. It's the first time I remember being really furious with a book, and realizing that I had no positive representations of Arabs in literature to counter it with.

Slightly more subtle than that was the moment towards the end of Greg Bear's *Songs of Earth and Power* where, with the Sidhe living openly among us, saving whales and preventing airplane crashes and the like, the following happens:

"Sidhe tribal sorcerers in the Middle East had been called upon by radical Moslems to raise the dead of past wars, that they might fight the Jews again. Human dead could not be literally resurrected, but the Sidhe had obliged by raising shadows and dreams of ancestors, breathing a kind of life back into the ghostly residues. These "dead" promptly occupied Arab villages, driving out the living and refusing to fight or do much of anything else. The Moslems had sworn vengeance."

After seven paragraphs of explaining how awesome is the world with the Sidhe in it, the above was the only example of a downside to their presence. After almost seven hundred pages of fantasy, Greg Bear lacked the imagination to conceive of a Middle-East without violence, in which "radical Moslems" aren't mucking things up by fighting "the Jews." That made me growly too.

I wanted to give a third example to round this out, and talk about Bill Willingham's *Fables*, but if I get started on that I might not ever stop.

Julia Starkey: I think *all* types of fiction are good ways to discuss racial issues, in that they are able to get to the heart of the story without factual details getting in the way.

Sf/f is a genre that relies heavily on worldbuilding. I think that the process of creating fictional universes lends itself toward rethinking how one's world works. Not being concerned about certain types of verisimilitude just makes that process easier.

One of the authors whose examination of racial issues deeply affected me was Tolkien. After reading Tolkien, I internalized as "normal" some less-than-ideal beliefs about race. I just knew that someone who was wise and wielded magic was likely to have pale white skin and long, straight golden hair. (They also statistically tended to be women.) I learned to be suspicious of the motives of swarthy people.

The compelling world that Tolkien created is in the background of many fantasy novels (especially high fantasy). Tolkien's racially essentialist beliefs are an inseparable part of the world he created. To be influenced by Tolkien's work is also to be influenced in some way by his beliefs about race. I grew up thinking that good people were just white, and dark races were just inherently debased and inferior. I've read hundreds, if not thousands, of books where uncivilized dark-skinned hordes come from the East, and where noble white men are destined to rule. It's impossible to underestimate the effect that has on a person.

Ursula K. Le Guin's writing, particularly the Earthsea books, have also dealt with race in a meaningful but more positive way. In Earthsea, heroes could have dark skin, and the West wasn't the only place that was civilized. Le Guin's stories struck an emotional chord with me. The ease and truth with which Le Guin dealt with different races and cultures has really stayed with me. When a white writer says that they don't know how to write about other cultures, I think of Le Guin. Her writing not only made a space for people who looked like me, but also for people who looked like some of my family and friends.

The two authors who have written about race in compelling and meaningful ways for me are Alaya Dawn Johnson and N.K. Jemisin.

Reading *Racing the Dark* by Johnson, I was blown away by how she flipped the script on what kind of people and culture should appear in a fantasy novel, especially a YA fantasy novel. In *Racing the Dark,* Johnson creates a world inhabited by a variety of races and ethnicities who are different from her own ethnic and racial background. I found *Racing the Dark* to be compelling and fresh because of the skillful way in which Johnson writes about the variety of cultures and social classes.

I read N.K. Jemisin's *One Hundred Thousand Kingdoms* while traveling to the International Conference on the Fantastic in the Arts. Jemisin is incredibly adept at incorporating diverse cultures into her world. I was so engrossed in the book that I didn't pay much attention to what was going on around me. This led to me first almost missing a bus to the airport, and later walking past the gate where my plane was going to be. The majority of fantasy books I browse don't come close to this level of connection and interest for me.

What I feel most often, as a person of color reading speculative fiction, is a sense of double consciousness (as in W.E.B. Du Bois, not psychic powers). The audience is almost always presumed to be white, and this can make my reading experience feel dissonant. Authors of speculative fiction consciously create characters who are meant to be perceived as exotic, but they unconsciously assume that all of their readers will share their own racial prejudices and privileges.

For example, if I'm reading a book with purple aliens, I have the experience of "ooh, exotic purple aliens!" At the same time, I can notice the characters act in ways that are based in my own society's racial stereotypes, reminding me that, to the author and their presumed audience, I'm the metaphorical purple alien. It's simultaneously thinking, "Oh no, dusky people from the desert are coming! They're terrifying!" and "Oh, right, people who have brown skin like me are scary because we're all living in a racist society. I guess I'll carry on." This can make me feel more acutely aware of being the "Other."

[Thanks to Marta S. Rivera Monclova, Kelly Mulligan,
and Tanya D. for helping me to explore this topic. J.S.]

Candra K. Gill: I don't know if I would say that science fiction and fantasy are particularly well or ill suited to examine racial issues as much as I would say that they're in a special position that, when taken advantage of, can lead to something interesting. Whenever I talk about this kind of thing, I usually point to the inherent "what if?" of speculative fiction in all its myriad forms. That "what if" beacon can be turned on racial issues as well or poorly as it can be turned on anything else. When it's done well, it can be anything from illuminating to exhilarating. When it's done poorly, it can come across as clumsy and naïve at best and offensive at worst.

As time goes by, I find myself less and less interested in heavy-handed allegory. For example, the kind that has aliens, or vampires or whatever, stand in as oppressed groups drives me up a wall nine times out of ten. Though this can be very well done, it mostly ends up feeling like a kind of side-stepping, especially when the whole of humanity is depicted as monocultural, or when the issues don't translate or map as well as the author thinks they do. Rather, I find myself more drawn to extrapolation and reflection. I like near- and far-future looks at human multicultural societies, for instance, that reflect upon historical and present societies and societal issues, without tipping into the Magical Utopia of Everything's Fine Now. I also like retellings of cultural stories and certain kinds of alternate or parallel history. At its best, this kind of work contextualizes racial issues in a way that allegories often fail to, because this kind of work is willing to deal with race as an issue head-on.

All of that said, speculative work doesn't necessarily have to deal with race directly in order to have important things to say about race. I'm glad that more and more writers of color who write about characters of color are getting published in the genre, for instance—though of course the field has a long way to go when it comes to representation and inclusion. There's something wonderful about visualizing ourselves in the future, regardless of whether or not race as an issue is a focus of a given story. It feels like a way of asserting ourselves in the present.

WisCon 34 "The Politics of Steampunk": Panel Report and Reflections

by Zola Mumford

Definition and complication

> Steampunk: a genre of science fiction that typically features steam-powered machinery rather than advanced technology. *Oxford English Dictionary. (Added 2010)*

Steampunk is neither simply nor quickly defined. If one approached writers, fans, con participants, and journalists with the question, "What is steampunk, precisely?", a wide variety of answers would result, one of them likely to be the response that there may not be a precise definition. Perhaps the variety of answers to the question complicates discussions within steampunk fandom about the subjects of race, racism, colonialism, inclusion of characters (or indeed real-life fans) of color, and nostalgia. In an ideal fandom, the good elements of the past (gadgets, fashion, fantastic narrative elements, aesthetic style) would be combined with modern technology to create a subculture free of racism (be it Victorian or modern) and as accessible to everyone as possible.

Desiderata

Steampunk fiction and objects are usually, with some exceptions, inspired by physical, cultural, aesthetic, and historical elements of nineteenth-century or Victorian-era Britain. Authors and fans may also draw from other historical periods and settings to create alternate histories. As a reader of speculative fiction, science fiction, and fantasy, I am intrigued by stories that stretch the geographic, aesthetic, and temporal boundaries of these genres. Many authors, including those who identify as people of color and those who do not, are already creating such challenging steampunk stories.

I remain curious about how far and wide the boundaries might go: for example, the inclusion of fantastical steampunk elements in stories about Chinese railway laborers in 1870s California, or African American inventor Garrett Morgan's secret blueprints—pushed to the back of a drawer—of inventions serving wildly different purposes than the traffic signal and gas mask for which he is primarily known. Maybe a homesick young Native American girl forced to stop speaking her first language at a government-run boarding school discovers her ability to manipulate mechanical objects in ways that appeal to her sense of self-preservation? A Latino teenager in 1920s Los Angeles participates in services at a mission led by an Aimee Semple McPherson-like evangelist, and notices that the church musicians and their instruments function a little too smoothly to be human? In an alternate version of the year 1854, a character based upon Antonios Bishallany, the first Lebanese immigrant to the United States, finds his adjustment to the new environment both eased and complicated by a bizarre contraption involving trans-Atlantic speaking tubes. Or perhaps a character resembling Harriet Tubman seriously considers an offer from an airship pilot to help her ferry Underground Railroad passengers to freedom.

The historical research needed to craft steampunk-inspired tales is a worthwhile and often entertaining effort. Following the panel report at the end of this brief essay I have included a bibliography and some historical resources to further the creation of these enticing sorts of stories. Many of these resources, such as digital archives, include images and text inclusive of people of color and information about colonization.

Current discourse

In *The Guide to Writing Fantasy and Science Fiction* (2010) Philip Athans and R.A. Salvatore quote Lev Grossman in *Time Magazine*: "The same way punk took back music, steampunk reclaims technology for the masses.... It maximizes what was miniaturized and makes visible what was hidden." Internet technologies have provided easier access to visual and text records of the lives of people of color; perhaps some authors may be inspired to use steampunk to make visible what was hidden or ignored about people of color.

And what of the political and social aspects of punk? In the *steampunkdebate* community on LiveJournal, LJ user "makeaneworld" posted the following comment to a July 2010 discussion of race and steampunk:

> I often think that the "punk" aspect of *Steampunk* gets overlooked a lot. It often seems that aesthetics that have been labelled "Steampunk" would sit more accurately under the label of "Victoriana". My take on Steampunk is that it should be *all about* challenging the contentious societal and cultural issues of the Age of Steam, about counterculture in the way that Punk was in the 70s. That rather than being swept under the carpet, the racism, sexism, classism etc. should be brought out in the open and examined in a critical but (hopefully) sensitive way. Or, y'know, blown to smithereens. *g* (If I ever get round to writing my Steampunk influenced novel, it will feature amongst others a trans person and a female Jewish airship captain.)

Both steampunk fiction and fan creativity acknowledge the role of science in Victorian popular culture, and the period's sense of wonder and discovery. As a result, steampunk fandom may appear on the surface to be overly involved with gadgets and fashion, ignoring historical, political, and social realities. Mass killings and physical violence against native peoples under colonialism, and legally enforced racial segregation were part of the time period in which steampunk stories are set. But what does wearing a pith helmet—even if the wearer claims to do so in an ironic, provocative fashion—indicate? Is it the wearer's ignorance of, indifference to, or even nostalgic desire for a return to the colonialism that the pith helmet represents? Does a nostalgic or idealized view of the past attract some fans to steampunk? Bloggers and essayists such as Jha (Jaymee Goh), Ay-leen the Peacemaker, and Evangeline Holland have addressed the issues of representation or absence of characters of color in steampunk. Jha and Ay-leen the Peacemaker have also written about participation by people of color in steampunk conventions, or cons.

Reporting

The panel "The Politics of Steampunk" was presented on May 29, 2010, at WisCon 34. Panelists were Liz L. Gorinsky (the moderator), an editor at Tor Books, and writers Amal El-Mohtar, Jaymee Goh (Jha), Theodora Goss, Piglet, and Nisi Shawl. Panelists spoke of their experience of participating in steampunk as fans, researchers, and authors.

The remarks that follow are reconstructed from my notes made as I listened in the audience. Some remarks are more obviously paraphrased, but probably none are exact. Questions and comments from the audience are included, and their names given when known.

Amal El-Mohtar: "In my fiction writing, I am playing with Victoriana in the way that Victorians played with medievalism. In popular culture, there seems to have been a shift from the popularity of 1980s medieval fantasy worlds to the steampunk aesthetic. There are parallels between our current age, the 2000s and 2010s, and the Victorian era; people are attracted to the possibilities of science, and there's a sense of wonder about technology. During the Victorian era people would tinker with things and were open to seeing what would happen. Many Victorian-era innovators recognized now as forward-thinking scientists were also occultists."

Theodora Goss: "The Victorian era included a fin-de-siecle and we are also living in one; societies are trying to figure out who they are and how we relate to things in our world, which is increasingly technologically complex."

Piglet: "Some of the appeal of steampunk is that people like being able to tinker with mechanical objects whose function is obvious."

Jaymee Goh quoted someone who had said that steampunk was a reaction to the presence of minorities in science fiction, a desire to return to a time when white expansion and colonization were dominant. She also quoted a thread on a white supremacist website where someone praised steampunk because it "returned power to white men."

Liz Gorinsky: "Does anyone have any thoughts on US and world politics, and how they may relate to steampunk?"

Piglet discussed the shifts, changes, and endings of empires and the resulting changes in post-colonialist countries.

Jaymee Goh: "We are not living in a post-racial America. The Victorian era was complicated and gritty and difficult racially."

Amal El-Mohtar: "From a Lebanese-Canadian perspective I cannot tell if there has been a change in the racial climate of the United States. Do Americans feel a need to articulate racial issues in a way that steampunk makes possible? Britain and the US have shaped the modern history of the Middle East, and I tend to view geopolitics from that point of view."

Theodora Goss: "Steampunk makes safe an era that was not safe. For some fans it involves nostalgia. Imagine doing more with steampunk; it could also be something that plays with, questions, and interrogates nostalgia. There's a narrative of the loss of empire and power in the current national political dialogue."

Liz L. Gorinsky asked panelists to address the resistance of the steampunk community to discussions of race and social issues.

Nisi Shawl: "One message I often hear is that the steampunk community just wants to have fun."

Jaymee Goh: "In a discussion within the LiveJournal steamfashion community, someone expressed the idea that it is fantasy and so there is no need to do any examination or analysis. There seems to be a lot of narrow thinking out there: 'If it's not set in Victorian England, it's not steampunk.' I suspect it's because steampunk is so overwhelmingly white."

Goh went on to discuss how she and a collaborator, Ay-Leen the Peacemaker, had given a presentation, "Envisioning a Better Steam Society: Social Issues in Steampunk" at the Steampunk World's Fair in Piscataway, New Jersey, a couple of weeks before WisCon 34. A woman who attended the presentation later told Goh and Ay-leen, "Well, I counted 27 Black people here." The number was mentioned in a way that suggested that such a "head count" was proof that the event was indeed diverse, though the event was attended by at least 3,000 people. (However, this approach does not take into consideration those who "pass"—people who may not look like "visible minorities" with certain skin tones, eye shapes, or hair textures.)

Goh also mentioned that she's used to being one of the few Chinese people at (science fiction and related) cons. She has observed that people seem to be invested in maintaining their fantasy and don't like people spoiling their fun; they jump thru a lot of intellectual hoops to avoid discussion.

Liz L. Gorinsky: "Do we actually have an awareness of race, gender, class, ageism, disability? What do we want to see more of in steampunk? What areas are we doing better in?"

Amal El-Mohtar: "Gender seems to get covered a lot more than anything else. Women participants in steampunk have the shiny toys and ray guns too. For readers seeking fictional works in the steampunk genre that provide a more complex view inclusive of people of color, I recommend anything by Shweta Narayan, who creates a sort of steampunk India." El-Mohtar would like to see less steampunk that is about "perceiving the other and more that is about being the other. I love the fact that a lesbian steampunk anthology is coming out." The anthology, *Steam Powered,* edited by JoSelle Vanderhooft (see bibliography), has been published since this panel took place.

Nisi Shawl found a short passage in Steven Barnes' alternate history novel *Zulu Heart* in which a young black girl invents the submarine. N.K. Jemisin's novelette *The Effluent Engine* is available online and in the *Steam Powered* anthology. Maurice Broaddus was recommended by Shawl and other panelists at this session; his website is at http://mauricebroaddus.com/.

Shawl mentioned that there was a graphic novel Jane Irwin was working on in which racial issues were addressed. "What I'm trying to say in about 80,000 words is that it's getting better," she added.

Piglet: "It is disturbing to see people walking around dressed like the image of the White Explorer (pith helmets, etc.); these are types of things we're seeing for sale by steampunk fashion vendors."

Theodora Goss: "How do you interrogate something through steampunk fashion? You see crossdressing, women dressed as Victorian gentlemen and so on. How do you interrogate issues of race and class though clothing?"

Liz L. Gorinsky mentioned a researcher who discussed steampunk regionalism. According to him, activities vary between cons. Steampunk convention attendees in some places like high tea. San Francisco likes

DIY objects and activities. At Dragoncon and other conventions, some fans are interested in Civil War reenactment steampunk.

Jaymee Goh stated that in her research she has noticed that some UK steampunks are using the steampunk culture to teach English history. She mentioned Conselo Steampunk, a Brazilian steampunk society. Goh finds that socioeconomic class is often addressed through steampunk fashion. Most people involved in cosplay or roleplay don't want to be the down-and-dirty mechanics. She has found that fans frequently play with gender; some women want to wear their Victorian style underwear on the outside, or to be the airship captain.

Goh remarked that she had seen more steampunk works acknowledging race recently. She cited John Mungo's *Virtuoso,* which depicts a technologically advanced Africa, and the online comic *Girl Genius,* which includes a few characters of color. She also noted: visual artist Yinka Shonibare's use of African-patterned, Dutch wax printed cloth to make Victorian costumes. People from colonized or immigrant cultures might use steampunk to try and place themselves, to create their own narrative, Goh said.

Amal El-Mohtar: "Steampunk narratives are often very Orientalist. There's a lot of othering already present in society, which can be reappropriated and played with. Why can't we be from these other places that are not England and play with them, and why can't that be steampunk as well?"

Theodora Goss: "People forget how many different ethnicities were living in Victorian England."

Amal El-Mohtar: "In much of the steampunk I've read, there's a sort of jingoistic loyalty to the monarchy, and any politics tend to be based in "secret societies," which were common in the Victorian era—many of them quite bizarre and involving cultural appropriation, such as the Society of the Noble Red Man."

El-Mohtar found it intriguing to imagine shifting the center of imperial power from England and thinking of the other empires of the world. She mentioned her interest in writing a novel set in the Middle East. "Imagine a Middle East that hasn't been colonized," she said. "There's the idea that North America has to bring democracy to the rest of the world, but there's also the idea that if you leave a country alone it will develop on its own, and develop its own social justice. That social justice may not look the way you expected it to. Steampunk authors don't need to create an amorphous nation within a work of fiction, but could imagine it having its own politics."

Nisi Shawl recommended fiction by Michael Swanwick, whose characters include a talking dog and a scam artist claiming to be from Russia; the scam artist plays upon Britons' perceptions of an empire different from Britain, and their ideas of what this other empire is like. Shawl discussed conducting historical research about groups of people who've been seen by their contemporaries as being in opposition to Victorian-era cultural and social norms. Shawl is researching and writing a steampunk novel set in the Belgian Congo; the characters include a group of Fabian Socialists and their attempt to create a Utopian colony.

Jaymee Goh: "Whatever fandom you get into, you meet a lot of people who...just don't want to think about or discuss these issues [of racism]. However, there are a lot of people who participate in steampunk and can do a lot of damage, and part of the reason I want to do work to make it more diverse is to prevent that. Right now things are looking up—you can have discussions. Some want to remain clueless, but others want to learn. So often a [person of color doesn't] have the energy to educate, to debate, but I am finding other ways to put out the information."

Amal El-Mohtar: "Most of the people I meet are really awesome, and I am aware that I am lucky to live in the wonderful, rarefied world of my LiveJournal friends list. I have found a kind, supportive segment of fandom with people who want to do things the right way."

Jaymee Goh talked about being among the panelists for "Envisioning a Better Steam Society: Steampunk & Social Issues," a roundtable discussion at the 2010 Steampunk World Fair. Goh and co-organizer Ay-leen the Peacemaker asked potential participants to RSVP for the roundtable; receiving only eight responses, they ordered only twenty cupcakes for the participants. On the day of the event, about 75 people showed up to participate in the roundtable discussion. Goh joked, "People were actually more interested in the discussion than the cupcakes." The roundtable went well and the responses were encouraging.

Liz L. Gorinsky said that as an editor at Tor Books she is excited to see progressive, inclusive steampunk submissions.

Theodora Goss: "You get seriousness in the literature when you engage with the culture. Maybe we're seeing the beginning of some sort of engagement with issues in steampunk. Nisi's novel sounds amazing because it's exactly the kind of novel that would do that."

Nisi Shawl: "Serious stuff can be serious fun."

Piglet remarked that it was good to hear all the optimism on the panel. She had earlier attended another con where most of the 2,000 vendors were selling steampunk items, up from about three vendors with steampunk items the previous year. There may be a gradual shift in steampunk; the DIY ethos may fade. Medievalism (popular during the Victorian Era) eventually became Disney princesses. She said that something similar may happen to steampunk.

At this point, questions and comments were accepted from the audience.

Audience member: "When considering all of the gadgets involved in steampunk, think about where the supplies to make them come from, where you get bronze and brass from. Gaskets: rubber from the Belgian Congo. Chemicals from the Middle East. Cotton from India. The Victorian world was supplied by colonies."

Jaymee Goh recommended Stephen Hunt's novel *The Court of the Air*, which deals with some of these issues. Goh also commented on DIY culture: "It's often expensive to build your own stuff, and it may be a sign of privilege that you can; but buying the stuff is also a sign of privilege." Goh said she'd met a person from the Crimea who didn't understand the fuss in US pop culture and youth culture about DIY because it was just "how we live in the Balkans."

Liz L. Gorinsky: "In many cities there are hacker spaces where people collectively own tools; when I needed a drill press to make something I used a Brooklyn hacker space."

Audience member: "There's an issue of romanticism. Some people see the Industrial Age as 'where we got it wrong' and steampunk is a re-imagining of getting it right. But we may be still getting it wrong."

Jaymee Goh discussed cultural appropriation and showed the audience a nonfunctioning bricolage gun she had created from a "tourist item," as she described it. Using a Balinese flute ("You should give credit to the people/culture you got it from," Goh said) carved in the form of a dragon, she added a handle, trigger, and other parts, and painted the gun silver. The flute itself was based on a traditional cultural item that is now mass-produced.

Amal El-Mohtar: "There is an opportunity for interrogation of material and cultural sources. In every sort of ugliness, there's an opportunity to rework and improve."

Audience member Moondancer Drake: "Are there recommendations for sites where someone would go to explore culturally sensitive steampunk?"

Jaymee Goh: "Your history books." (Audience laughter.) "Blogs such as *beyondvictoriana.com* are essentially restating what they've found in history books." Goh said she does the same in her own blogging. Steampunk, especially multicultural steampunk, is still so new that there are fewer resources [than there are for other fandoms].

Theodora Goss: "Some people are looking back to the 1880s and asking 'Where did we go wrong?' Steampunk is looking back to Victorian literature more than the era itself in some ways, and we should bear in mind that the literature itself is bending the truth through interpretations."

Jaymee Goh described the reaction of some steampunk fans to an image created by the Disney corporation showing its famous characters dressed in steampunk style. She remarked that blogger Cory Gross (*Voyages Extraordinaires*) noted how many steampunk fans were themselves influenced by Disney's interpretations of machinery and the Victorian era and other historical periods in films and cartoons.

Audience member: "I am active in SCA (the Society for Creative Anachronism) and we're trying to improve awareness around Orientalism and other problems in costuming and cosplay. I think that we should address people who are dressed offensively. People are reimagining costuming and finding other ways to present themselves."

Panel members thanked the audience for their participation and the panel concluded.

Appendix: Resources for Steampunk Writers and Artists

A. Articles, blog posts, essays, and other writing

B. Blogs

C. Image databases

D. Media, eBooks, and other resources

A. Articles and blog posts

Ay-leen the Peacemaker. "'From the Wilds of America'—Analyzing the Idea of 'British Colonial America' in Steampunk." *Racialicious.com*. July 2009, <http://www.racialicious.com/2009/07/01/%E2%80%9Cfrom-the-wilds-of-america%E2%80%9D-%E2%80%93-analyzing-the-idea-of-%E2%80%9Cbritish-colonial-america%E2%80%9D-in-steampunk-essay/>. Internet resource.

Barnes, Steven. *Zulu Heart.* New York: Warner Books, 2003. Print.

Goh, Jaymee. "The Roundtable of DOO- I mean, of Race and Steampunk." *Tor.com*. October 27, 2009, <http://www.tor.com/blogs/2009/10/the-roundtable-of-doo-i-mean-of-race-and-steampunk>. Internet resource.

Holland, Evangeline. "Anti-racism in 19th century Britain." *BeyondVictoriana.com*. June 13, 2010, <http://beyondvictoriana.com/2010/06/13/beyond-victoriana30-anti-racism-in-19th-century%C2%A0britain%E2%80%93guest-blog-by-evangelineholland/>. Internet resource.

Hunt, Stephen. *The Court of the Air.* New York: Tor, 2008. Print.

Jemisin, N.K. The Effluent Engine. January 19, 2010, <http://nkjemisin. com/2010/01/a-story-for-haiti-the-effluent-engine/>. Internet resource.

Jha. "Steampunking: Are Steampunk Westerns Non-Eurocentric? No." *Racialicious.com*. November 11, 2009, <http://www.racialicious. com/2009/11/11/steampunking-are-steampunk-westerns-non-eurocentric-no/>. Internet resource.

Jha. "The Intersection of Race and Steampunk: Colonialism's After-effects and other stories from a Steampunk of Colour's Perspective." *Racialicious.com*. 24 June 2009, <http://www. racialicious.com/2009/06/24/the-intersection-of-race-and-steampunk-colonialisms-after-effects-other-stories-from-a-steampunk-of-colours-perspective-essay/> Internet resource.

La Ferla, Ruth. "Steampunk Moves Between Two Worlds." New York Times. 8 May 2008, <http://www.nytimes.com/2008/05/08/fashion/08PUNK.html>. Internet resource.

makeanewworld. Posted reply to "Hello, New Members." Steampunkdebate LiveJournal community. July 4, 2010, <http://community.livejournal.com/steampunkdebate/11156. html?thread=225940#t225940>. Internet resource.

Narayan, Shweta. "The Mechanical Aviary of Emperor Jalal-ud-din Muhammad Akbar." *Steampunk II: Steampunk Reloaded*. San Francisco, CA: Tachyon, 2010. Print.

Vanderhooft, JoSelle (ed.) *Steam Powered*. Round Rock, TX: Torquere Press, 2011.

VanderMeer, Ann, and Jeff VanderMeer. *Steampunk II: Steampunk Reloaded*. San Francisco, CA: Tachyon, 2010. Print.

B. Blogs, Web sites, and Online Forums

This is by no means intended to be a comprehensive list of steampunk sites or blogs relevant to the subject of race and steampunk. This list does include blogs or online communities in which issues of race, colonialism, and ethnic diversity have been acknowledged and discussed.

AfroCyberPunk   http://afrocyberpunk.wordpress.com/
While not writing about steampunk per se, blogger Jonathan Dotse, based in Accra, Ghana, does address science/speculative fiction, alternative futures, and the DIY ethos.

Beyond Victoriana   http://beyondvictoriana.com
Ay-leen the Peacemaker and guest posters present "inclusive as opposed to exclusive analysis, book reviews, and steampunk news." "This is a blog about multicultural steampunk and retro-futurism—that is, steampunk outside of a Western-dominant, Eurocentric framework. All of the steampunkery here focuses on non-Western cultures, underrepresented minorities in Western histories (Asian/Pacific Islander, Middle Eastern, First Nation, Hispanic, black/African), and the cultural intersection between the West and the non-West."

Carl Brandon Society   http://www.carlbrandon.org
As this Web site states: "The mission of the Carl Brandon Society is to increase racial and ethnic diversity in the production of and audience for speculative fiction." Resources include a discussion list and a wiki for speculative fiction authors and characters of color.

Costume Mercenary   http://costumemercenary.blogspot.com/
Blog managed by Jeanette Ng. The focus is on costume creation, materials, and general creativity.

Silver Goggles: http://silvergoggles.blogspot.com/
Jaymee Goh's blog. Silver goggles are worn "by the steampunk postcolonialist when engaging with issues of race, representation, diversity, and other such exciting adventures as one might find in a Scientific Romance."

Steampunk Debate   http://community.livejournal.com/steampunkdebate/
A moderated forum welcoming steampunk enthusiasts to "a place to civilly discuss Steampunk and the ideas behind it." The 2010 description included this statement: "You may run into people with whom you disagree, and I am going to ask you to talk and debate—but when it's done, you may have to agree to disagree.

That said...hate speech, persistent racist and sexist speech, will get you banned. (I am willing to give folks the benefit of the doubt, we all say dumbass, ignorant or unintentionally hurtful things from time to time. Say your Mea Culpas, and we can move on.)" A July 2010 discussion included comments on "Oriental" costuming.

Tor.com
Since 2010, Tor.com has published posts on the subject of race and steampunk by speculative fiction and science fiction authors and essayists.

C. Image databases

Digital Librarian   http://www.digital-librarian.com/images.html
This site guides users to online digital archives and online image collections throughout the world.

Dutch Nationaal Archief   http://www.flickr.com/photos/
nationaalarchief
Images of colonial life in Indonesia and elsewhere; photos of historically significant events and everyday life in the Netherlands. There are many images of unusual gadgets. Go to the Flickr group to browse photos, or see images of maps and documents: http://www.en.nationaalarchief.nl/. The "Farewell to the Indies" section includes documents related to Japanese occupation, the Bersiap Period and the decolonization of the Netherlands East Indies.

Library of Congress Digital Preservation Partner Collections http://
www.digitalpreservation.gov/collections/collections.html
"Preservation partners from around the world are selecting and preserving at risk digital content. Use this interface to explore what has been collected so far." Includes audio, video, geospatial, text, image, and other types of content.

Library of Congress Prints and Photos Online Catalog
                         http://www.loc.gov/pictures/
"The Prints and Photographs Online Catalog (PPOC) contains catalog records and digital images representing a rich cross-section of still pictures held by the Prints and Photographs

Division and, in some cases, other units of the Library of Congress, begins this site's long self-description.

"The Library of Congress offers broad public access to these materials as a contribution to education and scholarship.

"The collections of the Prints and Photographs Division include photographs, fine and popular prints and drawings, posters, and architectural and engineering drawings. While international in scope, the collections are particularly rich in materials produced in, or documenting the history of, the United States and the lives, interests and achievements of the American people." A basic keyword search of the Library of Congress Prints and Photographs online catalog may produce thousands of images of Native Americans in real or posed situations, stereographic images of Lebanon and Syria, nineteenth and early twentieth century images of African Americans, images of urban and rural life from a wide variety of historical periods, or a drawing of Chinese New Yorkers looking up at the moon on Mott Street in New York City in 1884.

Research Buzz   http://www.researchbuzz.org/r/
This site describes itself as "News about search engines, digital archives, online museums, databases, and other Internet information."

World Digital Library   http://www.wdl.org/en/
"The World Digital Library (WDL) makes available on the Internet, free of charge and in multilingual format, significant primary materials from countries and cultures around the world," per the site's self-description.

D. Media, eBooks, and other resources

Freesound
Would listening to clips of a wooden threshing machine, various steam engines, ticking and chiming antique clocks, or a ship's bell help you to write a scene? The Freesound Project describes itself as "a huge collaborative database of audio snippets, samples, recordings, bleeps" and more. Many of these user-contributed sound-effect clips may be of interest to someone creating

steampunk-related content or performance works. The site is devoted to collecting sounds, not songs, although one may find samples of sounds made by such musical instruments as the accordion, piano, pump organ, and other instruments popular during the Victorian era. There are some recordings of antique music boxes. This content, although it may be downloaded for free, is licensed under the Creative Commons Sampling Plus License and the producers of each clip should be credited.

Project Gutenberg   http://www.gutenberg.org
Authors researching the experiences of Victorian-era people of color can download free eBooks from Project Gutenberg in over 60 languages; relevant works range from novels to history to biographies to cookbooks to reports on rural life in the Southern United States. With regard to the technology of the era, many general works dealing with machinery, science, and medicine are available. Some are illustrated. Writing about a different period? Project Gutenberg offers Medieval, 18th century, and 20th century works. Project Gutenberg is a nonprofit global project; donations are encouraged. Works include early twentieth-century sf-flavored pulp fiction such as *Tom Swift and His Airship* (1910) and an increasing number of 1950s-era science fiction; Marion Zimmer Bradley's *The Planet Savers* is a recent addition to the collection. Many of the books available here are travelogues detailing the authors' observations in countries under colonial rule. In addition to details about social and economic life, these works may include informative examples of ethnic and gender stereotypes, providing background about the social climate your characters might experience, and perhaps inspiring you with ideas about subverting those stereotypes.

The Dirigible of Dreams:
Steampunk, Race, Histories, and Visions of Inclusivity

by Jaymee Goh

Sometime in the midst of RaceFail2k9, I internet-met Ay-Leen the Peacemaker, who had written a post on being a steampunk and being Asian at the same time. It was posted to her MySpace blog, specifically written for the first Asian Women Blog Carnival. She discussed, eloquently, subjects resonating deeply with me: the feelings of alienation one could get when attempting to incorporate a non-white identity into a role-playing subculture very much centered on whiteness, the exoticization and Orientalism that participants in that subculture often indulge in, and the possibility of envisioning forms of steampunk that could include more of the world. She made the call, "Help me build them," and posted her email address publicly, so I took the chance to get in touch immediately.

We exchanged many emails covering all sorts of race-and-steampunk-related topics, and although we didn't meet in the flesh until much later, we got a lot of work done almost right away: we both wrote posts for *Racialicious* on being a steampunk of color and the general issues surrounding the subculture, which in turn scored us the chance to write for Shira Tarrant's upcoming anthology, "Fashion Talks." Ay-leen and I discussed creating a POC-only steampunk space and the necessity of exploring avenues of alternate-history jump-off points beyond Victoriana—she wanted to create a weekly feature on her Dreamwidth blog for that. When Torie Atkinson, then the blogmistress for *Tor.com*, asked me to write for Tor's *Steampunk Fortnight*, I casually mentioned the project. From this connection *Silver Goggles*, my blog exploring postcolonialism in steampunk, and *Beyond Victoriana*, Ay-Leen's resource for non-white steampunking, were born.

Steampunk, with all its conceits of anachronism, retro-futurism, and alternate history, has been Eurocentric, or rooted in literary traditions derived from Western European sources transplanted into U.S./Canadian America. In the 2008 *Steampunk* anthology edited by Ann and Jeff VanderMeer, Jess Nevins traces the history of the genre back to the dime novels of the 19th century, in particular the Edisonade, a subgenre wherein the protagonist was often a lone male scientist using the power of technology to have brilliant adventures. He was sometimes rich with a rags-to-riches story; he was rarely non-white. As a result of this history, there is often an assumed white-centric perspective in steampunk. Cory Gross of the blog *Voyages Extraordinaires* (http://voyagesextraordinaires.blogspot.com/) traces steampunk back to Scientific Romances of the Victorian and Edwardian eras. Both ancestries root steampunk in Europe, or European colonization and conquest. This carries over from the literature to the aesthetic, and from the aesthetic into role-playing performance. If you mosey into a steampunk site like *Steampunk Empire*, you'll find women dressed in Victorian-inspired outfits with corsets, bustles, lace, and frills (often adapted from goth and gothic-Lolita fashions). Men affect tweed jackets, vests, waistcoats, and the like. There is no shortage of Ladies and Barons, Lords and Captains, and the odd Professor. Then there are sartorial expeditions along middle- and lower-class lines: grubby mechanics and pirates, soldiers and explorers, and of course, the quintessential scientist.

The most powerful empire we can find the most information on, and which utilizes the technology that lends steampunk its name, is British. Hence, costuming and accessorizing involve a range of fashions from that era. White or non-white, this assumption tends to be the first made by most newcomers to steampunk. Most steampunk media and communities focus on Eurocentric fashions and histories, leading many potential non-white fans to assume it is not a subculture or subgenre for them.

Why, for example, would I want to get my Malaysian culture all up in that great civilization's history? I could watch, could consume, but there would be little for me to contribute.

Because steampunk is a very visual culture, I had other problems: making props and costumes is a time-consuming and resource-heavy hobby. As a student moving from place to place, not having grown up in an environment where I was encouraged to create things with my hands, I was at a loss as to how to proceed with no large workshop space and a minimum of materials. Moreover, a couple of stark realizations that my Asian appearance made a difference in how others perceived me and how I perceived myself made steampunk even less comfortable for me.

Jaymee Goh at Steampunk World's Fair in 2010. Jaymee describes her costume thus: "Wrap-around blouse from Bali, ordinary long-sleeved shirt, shorts, funky socks, and appropriately brown boots. The skirt was frankensteined from a ballgown bought second-hand; I split the back-zip seam for a coat-like flare. Parasol courtesy of the Shady Emporium." Photo courtesy of knightmare6.

For those of us who are non-white and yet wish to participate in steampunk, this raises several questions: why are we drawn to the aesthetic? What does our predilection for a colonizer's culture say about us? For those of us already ambivalent about our own "ethnic" heritages, does our indulgence in this fashion signify a devaluing of our ethnicity? Compound this with the fact that many of my adolescent years were filled with accusations from elders on how "Westernized" I am. What would people think if I were to trot about wearing Victorian English clothing? Did I want to betray my heritage further? And even if I did want to explore alternative accoutrements, they would be "Oriental;" as I learned more about Orientalism, my discomfort in adapting steampunk gear with elements from my culture grew: if I drew on Asian aesthetics for my steampunk outfit, did I Orientalize myself? Did I box myself in for the Western gaze? Would I be playing into Orientalist tropes and remaining trapped there? Would I get to have a speaking role and be an actor in my own story, with an audience that would understand where I was speaking from?

These questions are not made simpler when we are told that it doesn't matter, that it's all about individual taste. "Wear what you like," I would have thought years ago. "It doesn't matter. Being Chinese or Malaysian shouldn't define who I am." If people looked at me askance then, I could have waved it off as me being outlandish, nonconformist. Why should I let norms dictate the forms my hobbies took? Were steampunk's aesthetic and forms derived from a cultural void, these questions would be irrelevant, but they were not. As a subculture, literary genre, or visual aesthetic, steampunk is very much tied to the mainstream, which, in U.S./Canada is very white; when exported to non-white regions, it is mostly irrelevant and gains popularity at a slower rate.

I had questions and concerns, but it didn't seem like steampunk as a genre, aesthetic, or subculture would address them. Steampunk roleplay and discussions seemed to reflect this too: the focus was on the tech, and who held the tech that shaped our world today. Victorian England and Western Europe. Like most historical re-enactors, everyone I saw from where I sat wanted to talk props and sewing. I didn't feel like being the jerk who ruined the conversation by pointing out how there were so few non-white people, by asking why we focused on such a problematic time period, by wondering why, if it was alternate history, we were still supposed to dress so nice and celebrate Empire? I kept silent because I knew what the answer would be—if I had so much trouble, why didn't I just go find another hobby?

Thus, POC and non-whites who wish to address these concerns find themselves isolated—unless, by lucky chance, they stumble upon each other on the Internet, as Ay-leen and I did. Friends' lists and blogs, linkspams and round-ups, forums and mailing lists, social networking sites—these all serve different purposes, and new possibilities open up every day.

Of course, these new possibilities also open up new concerns: things I thought were unproblematic, and really are unproblematic when occurring within non-white spaces like Malaysia, were incredibly problematic in white-dominated spaces; things such as white people wearing "ethnic" costumes, or writing non-white characters. Given whole new contexts with different histories from those which I associate with such acts, I learned that there are things which are completely normal or novel to me, but which hurt others. For example, until RaceFail09 I'd never considered what cultural appropriation meant, much less how it is used to marginalize non-white peoples in white-dominant spaces.

The current trend towards "irony" adds an even more worrisome aspect to the atmosphere of popular culture's interface with steampunk. Those who follow this trend spout problematic remarks while presuming the audience at large will understand that "it's just a joke;" they thus expect to maintain a facade of such enlightenment that no one could ever accuse them of exercising their privilege.

Non-whites who internalize such attitudes as normal and acceptable lend credence to the idea that critique is unnecessary, oversensitive, and alienating. Already there have been examples of Orientalism within the steampunk subculture, most notably in the steamfashion LiveJournal community which uses an "Oriental" tag for Eastern-inspired steampunk and the introduction of the neologism "Victorientalism" by the editor of the *Gatehouse Gazette*. An outcry against the latter elicited defensive posturing of the desire to maintain romantic imaginings of the Orient "as it never was"—an exercise in creative nostalgia unfettered by acknowledgement of its inherent racism.

When I heard the *Gatehouse Gazette* was to release a "Victorientalism" issue in March '10, I felt I had to speak out. Bolstered by my friendship with Ay-Leen as well as other members of the steampunk community such as Allegra Hawksmoor and Jake von Slatt, I wrote a screed describing what Victorientalism is and why it was so problematic, meant as a 101 how-to that future steampunks could use when they encountered the term. RaceFail having happened only a year before, support was tremendous, and the pushback was almost comical, as the *Gazette's* editor, Nick Ottens, defended his position, and the contributors to the Victorientalism issue felt the need to defend their decision to associate with the *Gazette*. To his credit, Ottens attempted to have a dialog, though using such age-old excuses as (to paraphrase) "Orientalists loved the Orient!" and "It's just fantasy!" while dismissing disagreements as "less nuanced." People holding his position continue to maintain their supposedly guilt-free enjoyment of Orientalist tropes.

Although these factors appear discouraging, the current state of steampunk as a genre and subculture make it a good space for postcolonial exploration. Steampunk, at the time of this writing, is experiencing a boom; meanwhile, detractors complain of its saturation in imperialist, colonialist tropes. In fact, that these problematic aspects are among the first things distant observers of steampunk see is even more reason for the traditionally marginalized to take a hand in shaping steampunk, to stage an intervention as it were, in order to prevent steampunk from descending into pitfalls that other speculative genres have fallen into.

The racism of historical narratives is clear and obvious to people of color in white-dominated spaces, and even to individuals with white privilege. We know what we are up against. Pulling from the experiences of mainstream antiracist organizations and movements (as mainstream as they can be, anyway), we have the tools available to us to critique manifestations of racism as they arise, from the overt to the covert, and to engage meaningfully with historical patterns that have led to the world's conditions.

Steampunk has two major conceits: anachronism and alternate history. These are useful starting points for newcomers to steampunk. Anachronism in steampunk usually manifests in the highly-advanced technology, mores, and fashions placed within what is generally accepted as a less-advanced time period, accelerating the technological prowess of that period to suit the steampunk's taste. Hence, rayguns in weaponry, women airship pirates, and massive, multifunctional toolbelts. The use of anachronisms in steampunk depends on imagining what the past would have looked like if our predecessors had access to the knowledge and some of the limited resources of today. Alternate history uses a similar concept, except instead of people in the past using knowledge of the future, creators in the present use their knowledge of the past to explore how events and patterns would have unfolded if certain decisions or opportunities had changed. Very often in steampunk, this alternate history involves the element of anachronism.

Due to the focus on steam technology (as evidenced by its name), steampunk tends to center around the era that most utilized and developed steam: the 19th century, which just so happened to be the height of European conquest and colonialism. As many assume historical distance from the events that set the world on its current course, they feel free to re-imagine the era as a more positive time: of change (capitalism!) and discovery (Darwin!), when visible progress was achieved (the Industrial Revolution!). Because of the cultural imperialism mentioned earlier, it is difficult to divorce British/Western European supremacy from historical narratives. However, with the rising prominence of antiracist activism alongside other fields of social justice, it is not impossible to dream of alternatives. In fact, there are very few reasons why we should not address stereotypes created and perpetuated in the past while refraining from creating new, equally-destructive ones (and none of those reasons are good ones; "It's just fantasy!" only takes us so far).

Steampunk is fascinating for many reasons, among them this genre's followers' curiosity about and love for history. Steampunks find themselves connecting between generations as younger participants outfit themselves with fashions that older people recognize. For many of Western European descent, this is a joyous reconnection with a history of great significance.

Unfortunately, too often it is assumed that people who do not share that cultural/historical background would find no similar gain in exploring their own histories. This is untrue and unfair, as it implies that narratives that do not have the same standards of success as the dominant one are not worth as much, and thus not worth owning. Marilyn French, after spending ten years compiling information for her four-volume book *From Eve To Dawn* says in her first preface, "I wrote this history because I needed a story to make sense of what I knew of the past and what I saw in the present." Similarly, those of marginalized histories can explore those histories to make sense of the past that led to our present. Doing this can connect us to our heritage and root us in an identity larger than ourselves, if that is what we want.

Jaymee Goh in her modified pinafore with Ay-Leen the Peacemaker at Steampunk World's Fair, 2010. Photo courtesy of Nate Buchman of IndieNate Digital Photography.

As Ay-Leen and I emailed back and forth possibilities for steampunk in Asia, I delved into the history of Malaya and its connection to China. At the time, I was smarting over the realization that my genre writing was whitewashed and contributed to a body of literature that favored whiteness. I had by this point in my life spent years away from Malaysia, long enough to gain the distance from my home culture necessary for self-definition. I was interested in steampunk, but torn sometimes by my attraction to it. I was fine as long as I didn't look into a mirror and realize how my non-white inheritance seemed to conflict with steampunk's generalized Eurocentrism. Steampunk being a visual subculture made it hard for me to ignore that one of me was not like the others.

I was not too interested in the high adventure or the mad science, but I knew I would be awkward in fashionable white society.

For whatever reason, it did not occur to me to turn to my home. That took meeting Ay-Leen, and a good thing it was, since she was the first person I ever met to incorporate her Asian heritage into her steampunk persona.[1] Seeing the work she had put into her persona, I realized I faced more challenges before I could begin to build my own steampunk world, my own dirigible of dreams, as it were.

First (and this process still goes on), I had to decolonize my mind. I had to confront how I think, and the fact that so much of who I am has been constructed by ideals that disadvantage me. I had to tease out where specifics began and universality ended, scrub out ideals of objective truth and replace them with the acknowledgement of subjectivities. I took note of the way I talked and expressed myself, who I imagined my audience was, and how I approached a subject. Sometimes it was as simple as dropping the word "Oriental" from my vocabulary as a substitute for "Asian." Most times, it was difficult—without mastery over any Chinese dialect, it's tough for me to get closer to my Chinese history and heritage. I often can't figure out whether what I know of Chineseness is really Chinese.

Second, I had to learn more about my identity—information hitherto ignored or disregarded as irrelevant, or trotted out as conversation pieces. I delved into Malaysian history again, reacquainting myself with names of historical figures: Raja Kecil, Parameswara, Sultan Makarram Shah, Captain Francis Light, Kapitan Yap. I had to do this in the full knowledge that a racist government was in charge of my education. I began to wonder about the stories I had never heard, like how Minangkabau women maintained matrilineality or how Pattani Thai got along with Malays and Hoklo. I wondered how the peranakan communities, descendants of Chinese immigrants from as early as the 15th century, were treated, how they got along, how much isolation they used to maintain their heritage, and how much of Malay culture they absorbed. I can see shadows of their stories in historical statistics gleaned from university library books.

Third was the challenge of deciding how universal my writing had to be. Knowing now that trying to be universal is a fallacy, that "normal" often means a very narrow, specific experience and that most English-language fiction used a white lens we all learned to look at ourselves through, I had to decide what it meant to me to resonate with others, and how to do that. (It would take me a longer while to realize that specificity does not necessarily lead to alienation.)

With that, I began work on my first steampunk universe. I initially thought of developing a persona as well, because the concept seemed so fun, but eventually I ditched it in favor of world-building and literature. There was, and still is, so much to explore, especially in my own background. Southeast Asia has a long history of trade, politics, and colonialism separate from that of Europe. In my region, the Southeast Asian Maritimes, referred to by the British as the Malay Archipelago and called Nusantara by the locals, much of the shared pre-British colonial history vacillates between fact and myth. Undeniably, though, steampunk could adapt to it. I threw a dash of anachronism—steam technology come to fruition from the notes of real-life Arabian inventors—into the scientific background, and a wrench into the history of the peninsula that is now West Malaysia—preventing British imperialism. I found a suitable Arabic word that could conceivably be used to refer to an airship—"rohani" (spiritual).

I already knew where on the official historical timeline I wanted to produce a rupture, to create a new world in which the British didn't have a stranglehold: on the Penang island colony founded by Captain Francis Light. (That island is also where my parents were born and raised.) At the time of this colony's founding, the British were focused on India, and Southeast Asia was a bit far off to invest in. What would have happened to Nusantara without that colony? Would Malaysia, a single country made of several states, each of them with their own history, exist as I know it now?

With these questions in mind I produced my first publishable piece of fiction, "Between Islands."[2] Researching the history of my region also brought me closer to home in spirit, if not in terms of actual geography. I constantly came up with exciting questions to ask. Sometimes I found no answers, which is saddening, and challenged me to approximate what might have been while remaining true to what I knew of the interethnic relationships, racial politics, and culture that I grew up in. Race and nationhood are constructs, but understanding my relationship to them enabled me to frame them in fiction and embrace the diversity my country likes to take pride in.

In addition, doing this research gave me more of a context with which to understand others in a similar-but-not-the-same position. This process couldn't have happened without the conversations started by RaceFail09, which led to my many conversations with Ay-Leen.

Our initial emails were long, with much speculation on how the politics of Asia would have changed if Western Europe's colonization had been scaled back. Both of us were still new-ish to steampunk: I to the subgenre, she to the subculture, though neither of us were strangers to writing and roleplaying. I first emailed Ay-Leen in late April 2009; re-reading our old emails and thinking about how my views and how we now operate makes me marvel at the amount of growth a person can undergo in so short a time. In early 2009, I felt steampunk was "frills and lace and idealizers of an awful past," and Ay-Leen had just discovered *Steampunk Magazine*. We liked the gritty feel of cyberpunk, but felt steampunk had more positivity to it. We both believed strongly that the political connotations of steampunk were important.

Nowadays I am more likely to focus on what steampunk *could be*, as opposed to the problems I currently see.

My careless mention of being a "steampunk of color" attracted the attention of *Racialicious* editor Latoya Peterson, who asked me to write an essay for her. Ay-Leen was also invited to contribute an essay on how North American white steampunks viewed "the colonies" of the 19th century in roleplay. Reader reception was tremendous. Our essays got linked everywhere. It seemed that secretly, people wanted to talk about race and racism in steampunk, even if only to reassure themselves that things were okay and no one they knew was "like that." When Shira Tarrant asked us to write an essay for *Fashion Talks*, I shelved my fantasy novel in favor of university libraries and more long email exchanges with Ay-Leen. It was around this time that I found out Ay-Leen's real-life name and we began instant-messaging.

Meeting Ay-Leen in person took place a year later, at Steampunk World's Fair, May 2010. There, we gave a presentation on steampunk that wasn't Victorian called "Steam Around the World," and hosted a roundtable discussion where we invited people to comment on specific topics. For "Steam Around the World" we had a PowerPoint presentation, and we rehearsed for it using GTalk's video chat function. James Ng, one of the artists we featured, sent little samples of his work for me to distribute.[3] We were pretty well prepared. But the way the round-table went surprised me.

Ay-Leen and I had set it up as an event on the Steampunk Empire Ning, sure that we would get at most 25 people to show up for it. We offered cupcakes to encourage attendance. We got eighteen confirmed attendees. This number didn't include our planned speakers, there to begin and fill in the conversation: Lucretia Dearfour, Ay-Leen's fiancée (who spoke to gender and transgender issues and incorporated Japanese elements into her outfit); Emilie Bush (who self-published her book *Chenda and the Airship Brofman*, written in response to a lack of female heroines in steampunk); myself (to speak to issues of race); and Jake von Slatt of *The Steampunk Workshop*, our "token straight white male" (and one of our most valued allies).

On the day itself, in a small presentation room, Ay-Leen and I arranged the chairs into a circle. We had a version of the Speaking Stick rule: discussions were to be facilitated by Admiral Chang, Ay-Leen's steamborg panda. No one could speak without his permission; we had to hold him before we could say anything. Armed with a fluffy panda, cupcakes, and cough drops (for me; I nursed a lost voice), we prepared to have a deep conversation on social issues in steampunk, beginning with class, moving on to gender, and finishing with race. We kept the classifications simple since we didn't know our audience.

We weren't prepared for just how many people came. The chairs filled up quickly, and attendees took to standing behind chairs or sitting in front of them. By the door, there was a crowd. Lucretia, sitting closest to the door, later reported that there were people standing in the corridor outside the door listening in. I sat on the floor, blissfully unaware of the crowd beyond those I could see; of those I could see, everyone was paying close attention to the conversation, with many tentative and insightful contributions.

There were other POC attending. Referring to British colonials in Malaya I said, "Many people don't realize that even after the colonizers have left our shores, they left behind other after-effects, economically and socially." Monique Poirier, Seaconke Wampanoag, rightly pointed out to me, "You keep saying the colonizers left your shores. I think you need to remember that for us, here, the colonizers never left." The whole room fell silent, leaving me to vocalize how most of us were probably feeling: "OH SNAP!" She had delivered a needful reminder.

As we were running over the time allotted to us, we moved (with our cupcakes) to the bar area, where attendees continued the conversation in various groups for much longer.

Buoyed by the success of the roundtable, I made my way to WisCon 34, to the "Politics of Steampunk" panel, moderated by Liz Gorinsky, whom I had met at Steampunk World's Fair. WisCon had not been part of my initial plan; it was only a little more than a week after Steampunk World's Fair, and I didn't feel I could justify two trips into the States. However, Deepa D. nagged me into attending, taking advantage of the Carl Brandon Society's Con or Bust fund, and signing up for a panel. With my father's blessing I took my first train trip across the United States from New Jersey to Wisconsin, stayed with a friend of my father's for a week, and got a ride into Madison with Steam Century's Captain Brennan. Two days later, I was safely ensconced in the Concourse Hotel, ready for WisCon 34.

It is rather hard to describe my WisCon experience without getting into fine details, from the POC dinner at the beginning of the weekend, to the daily panels, to the meals in between and chats with others, to the nightly parties that I promised myself I wasn't going to go to but ended up at anyway. I sat on two panels: "Strangers Writing Strange Lands," and "The Politics of Steampunk." The latter was especially important to me: steampunk was booming, but nobody quite knew what it was. The visual aesthetic had gotten emphasized to the point of superficiality. The DIY ethic mashed and merged with crude capitalism. And of course, it was very, very white.

For some reason I felt it necessary to dress up for the occasion. I had two outfits: a modified pinafore, and a collection of pieces to approximate the syncretism of Victorian and Southeast Asian fashion. I went with the pinafore, which I'd bought several years ago for Halloween and found to be a comfortable summer outfit. The pinafore is among the many Western accoutrements that the Malaysian school system retained after colonialism, and it is worn mostly by non-Muslim students.

When modifying the pinafore as a steampunk costume I lined the front sides with dragon-shaped ornaments from a craft store (found in a cutesy section called "Oriental"; sometimes one has to work with what one's got), and the back with chain. On the waistline at the back I put a large ribbon made of several layers of tulle, to approximate a bustle. I added a pseudo-cravat made of a scarf, a ring with an obnoxiously large faux-pearl, and rubber bands and a choker tucked under the collar of an appropriate lacy blouse. And of course, I had a badly-made handcannon: while in Bali, I'd bought a dragon flute made for tourists, attached pieces of a plastic gun and spray-painted it silver. (I was also hoping Liz Gorinsky would dress up, because she had worn a fabulous outfit at Steampunk World's Fair, but alas, I was the only over-dressed panelist.)

Jaymee Goh toting the bricolage "handcannon" described above.

I don't remember much about the panel, except that I wanted to talk—about the literature and about the potential for POC in steampunk. I was also very intimidated and anxious, because Liz Gorinsky was the moderator, and because one of my co-panelists was Nisi Shawl, whose work *Writing the Other* Ay-Leen and I had referred to several times.

I had rather forgotten that steampunk didn't have a central hub, a single starting point, or an established canon. I was also very unused to doing without the mediation of text. Looking at the audience I realized I was speaking to fellow fans and writers of color who supported my work and understood the problems steampunk presented without my needing to explain them. It was a bit discombobulating to move my discourse to another level.

Needless to say, I left WisCon 34 happy and prepared to take on the conversation in more formal settings, like graduate school.

I have since reached out to more people about steampunk, such as Jeff VanderMeer, editor of steampunk anthologies, and Jess Nevins, author of *The Encyclopedia of Fantastic Victoriana*. I have also published two short stories set in a steampunk Southeast Asia. Everywhere I hear more ideas about non-Euro steampunk stories, such as Amal El-Mohtar's Syrian-based universe that runs on crystal technology, and Nisi Shawl's project of steampunking the Belgian Congo. Ay-Leen has won the Last Drink Bird Head Award for her work on *Beyond Victoriana*, which continues to highlight lesser-known histories so as to multiply the potential universes we can inhabit. Through our remembrance of the distant past we rewrite narratives, restructure systems, and represent the underrepresented. We have come so far; we have so much further to go. This dirigible of dreams is ready for its next upgrade: greater engine efficiency for the long journey ahead.

Endnotes

1. It is an observation of mine that Asian-Americans have found it necessary to balance belonging to the white-dominant American society and non-white heritages. This was not a problem of mine growing up, when I was steeped in non-white culture, which might explain why this solution Ay-Leen arrived at never occurred to me before meeting her.

2. Originally written for *Crossed Genres'* Eastern month, "Between Islands" found a home in *Expanded Horizons'* nineteenth issue.

3. James Ng's "Thought Process" is the cover art for this book.

Conversation About the *Avatar* Panel

by Neesha Meminger and Ibi Zoboi

Panel: Race and Gender in *Avatar*

Panelists: Annalee Newitz, Terry Bisson, E. Cabell Hankinson Gathman, Nick Murphy, Nnedi Okorafor

> About *Avatar* (this synopsis was taken from The Internet Movie Database at www.imdb.com): When his brother is killed in a robbery, paraplegic Marine Jake Sully decides to take his place in a mission on the distant world of Pandora. There he learns of greedy corporate figurehead Parker Selfridge's intentions of driving off the native humanoid "Na'vi" in order to mine for the precious mineral scattered throughout their rich woodland. In exchange for the spinal surgery that will fix his legs, Jake gathers intel for the cooperating military unit spearheaded by gung-ho Colonel Quaritch, while simultaneously attempting to infiltrate the Na'vi people with the use of an "avatar" identity. While Jake begins to bond with the native tribe and quickly falls in love with the beautiful alien Neytiri, the restless Colonel moves forward with his ruthless extermination tactics, forcing the soldier to take a stand — and fight back in an epic battle for the fate of Pandora.

Neesha Meminger: What were your views of *Avatar* before and right after you saw the film?

Ibi Zoboi: I'm a writer with three children, so I don't do twenty dollar movies (the price for 3D in New York, or close to it) unless they promise an apotheosis of some kind. That's exactly what *Avatar* gave me.

NM: I went in fully expecting to hate it. No one was more surprised than I when I came out not only *not* hating it, but maybe even actually liking it. And when I waited for my partner outside afterward, I caught some of the comments from the other people who'd been in the theater. One white woman was letting out a scathing stream of commentary into her cell phone— "Oh, my god, Leslie, it was horrible. Just horrible. It was *so* depressing. They were killing all the people and just tearing everything to pieces! I couldn't stand to watch anymore. Why would they let a film like this into the theaters?"

It dawned on me that this woman was upset because she actually saw the devastation and destruction most indigenous peoples have had to endure—up close. Closer than she would ever choose to be. In other words, if she had a choice—and most white people do—she would never, ever, put herself in a situation where she had to witness the pain and the complete demolition of people's homes and lives by invaders who looked just like her. Invaders who could've been her ancestors...her family. For me, it was exhilarating to witness that destruction, destruction I've seen over and over throughout my life—both on a personal level, in documentaries, historical texts, and throughout my family narrative—with an ending that depicted the conquered rising up and driving out the invaders.

So, what did you expect from the panel?

IZ: Well, WisCon is known to be more left of center than most cons. So I, of course, expected a love fest of all things *Avatar*. Maybe there would've been an in-depth analysis of all the environmental, racial, cultural, sexual motifs in the movie. I was eager to hear all the perspectives on how great *Avatar* was. But that's not what happened.

NM: Wow! See, my experience was the complete opposite. I had read all the online critiques of the movie, the *Dances with Wolves* comparisons, etc., and I had expected to hate the movie. But when I walked out *not* hating it, I was really disconcerted. I had to do a lot of searching around in my psyche for *why* I liked it. Was I hooked into some unexamined internalized racism?

How could I like this film that so many of my respected peers found objectionable? I'd done years of antiracism work, read all the tomes, revered authors like James Baldwin, bell hooks, Audre Lorde. How could I possibly *like* this film made by James Cameron, of all people??? And I'd hated *Dances with Wolves!*

So I wasn't planning to go to the *Avatar* panel, because I had a sense beforehand that it would mostly be a critique of the film a la *Dances with Wolves*—white man goes into foreign land, falls in love with a "native" woman, learns natives' ways, wins them over, then saves them. And all of that is absolutely true, but I wanted a more nuanced discussion. I wanted to talk about the complexities, and I wasn't convinced we'd have that conversation. It wasn't until Nnedi said, during our lunch, that she'd be on the panel and that she guessed hers would not be a popular opinion (she, too, didn't hate *Avatar*), that I decided to go. That's when I thought we might delve into some more interesting discussion.

IZ: There were five panelists, including authors Terry Bisson and Nnedi Okorafor. One of the panelists was very vocal about all the flaws in *Avatar*. The idea that *Avatar* was another "white man as savior" and "noble savages" movie was thrown around, and I get that. And I disagree. Not to say that those elements didn't exist in the movie. But what *Avatar* has done is place the brainpower behind indigenous cultures front and center—ancestral worship, communing with the environment, matriarchal society. And this is what I think most people of color were able to grasp from the movie and claim as their own.

NM: Exactly! Those were some of the points I had hoped to touch on. The fact that so much of the film encompassed elements that I, personally, had never seen on the big screen before. All of the spirituality, matriarchal power, etc., that you mention, Ibi, as powerful, positive elements—this is stuff I've longed to see reflected back to me throughout my life. For me, that aspect was a breath of fresh air. And I left the theater feeling like that was not all Cameron's work up there. He *had* to have had the input (massive input, I would say) of people of color, indigenous peoples, women. I don't have faith in his sensibility (I've seen his track record) enough to believe that *Avatar* was completely his brainchild. "Terminator" was not completely his, either, and I loved that film, too.

IZ: I don't know if those who were opposed to the movie understood when Nnedi and you said that you were able to see yourselves in the Na'vi. I think what we mean is that we were able to see the breadth and depth of our culture. There was a civility of sorts in how indigenous societies conducted themselves—it was noble, yes. But the savagery piece was from the perspective of an outsider who could not understand its complex system. So the larger metaphor was the humans' study of Pandora as this object that had to be dissected and studied. It was something that Jake Sully, a human studying the inhabitants of Pandora, had to be initiated into. Whether Native American, African, Indian—people of color who related to the Na'vi on some level understood that this is the tradition they come from. That we're way more than just savages doing rain dances and praying to trees. Our stuff is deep.

NM: I agree. And I could appreciate these things at the same time as critiquing the fact that this is a Cameron-made film, out of Hollywood, big budget, mainstream, usual tropes.

The one bit that gave me pause, however, was audience member Claire [Light]'s critique. Her comments were dead on. I'm going to do my best to summarize, and I hope I get it right, but basically Claire said that historically, leaders of revolutionary movements were always from within. Ghandi, Lumumba, Mandela—all were born and bred in the lands they later struggled to free. They went outside of their homes to learn the ways and styles of combat of the colonizers/conquerors, but then they came back home to free their people. The savior was never an outsider, someone from among the conquerors who "turned native" and then led the people to victory.

This was a bit of a stumper for me because it was bang on the money. And there was no arguing with it. It was something I needed to go away and think about because, even though I had known about Ghandi and Lumumba and Mandela, had watched films about their lives and read biographies and done research on their movements, none of that entered into my consciousness as I left the theater after watching *Avatar*. Why not? Why wasn't I incensed?

After much thought, I realized that while that point is absolutely, undeniably true, there was something else the movie gave me—a kind of hope; not a lot, mind you, but a tiny flicker, maybe. There were messages and values in that film that I've spent most of my life fighting to bring into wider consciousness. Messages and values that have been espoused by women, people of color, LGBTQ folks, and other "otherized" voices the world over. Messages and values that have been relegated to the margins, to silence, and driven underground. The idea that oppressed indigenous people, with less-advanced killing machines, could emerge victorious and drive out their oppressors; the idea that women can fight and be military equivalents to their male counterparts; that collective action can be valued over individual conquest, that working *with* Nature is more desirable than owning it or controlling it...these are precious concepts to me, and for once, I saw them splashed all over a giant screen, in 3D, in New York City. And I knew millions of other people would see them. Whether these people would really "get" it—well, that's another conversation. But the fact that some/any of these concepts had made it into the mainstream was refreshing.

I do think we'll always need to work together with our allies toward any kind of real justice and equality. And this film was about that for me on a very small, baby-steps level—not in the narrative necessarily, but in the fact that Cameron and his production team worked with all kinds of people in bringing this film and its ideas into the mainstream. It's a teeny-tiny step in getting people to change their thinking. In venturing into new ways of viewing the world. We're fighting on a global level, really—it's about ideas, and swaying the minds and psychologies of people. I think that was the appeal of the film for me, and why I was able to like it despite the usual Hollywood white-male-savior tropes.

IZ: Ah, you're much more optimistic than I am. Not to say that I disagree; however, I viewed *Avatar* from a more historical perspective. Certainly the movie does carry a message of hope, but I can't help but think that what happened to Pandora and the Na'vi has already happened to countless groups of people all over the globe. It's sobering to realize that in reality, there was no Hollywood happy ending. I'm sure that small battles were won here and there. But the very fact that we're here writing and speaking in English is a testament to our ancestors' defeat by the British, French, Portuguese, etc. What would've happened if there had been no Jake to save the Na'vi? Sure the Lumumbas fought the good fight; their efforts were not in vain. The truth of the matter is that ultimately, those with the bigger machines now have the upper hand, and they did this on the backs of billions.

        So instead of asking if this is an accurate depiction of native peoples' struggle, the larger question on the part of the oppressors ought to have been, "What have we done?" What infrastructures have been broken in wiping out whole cultures and societies? What is the result of disconnecting people from their rituals and traditions? I think people can think about these things on a global level, but there are little Pandoras being destroyed on a daily basis in the form of gentrification, in education, in the publishing and entertainment industries, etc., without any thought to the larger ramifications. And the panel had a lot to say on James Cameron as the person behind the magic. I'm not one to kill the messenger, but I can't help but wonder how *Avatar* would've been received had it been the brainchild of a person of color. Needless to say, *Avatar* and all other movies and books that examine our world with a fresh perspective (and this is best done in the form of fantasy or science fiction, I think) are a step in the right direction.

NM: Absolutely true. The entire reason *Avatar* was as big as it was is because Cameron's name was on it. Period. There is no way a film like this could have been made, on that scale, by a POC. The money and resources are only one factor. But the facts, that it *did* have those resources behind it and it *does* bear Cameron's name—those are the very reasons it is being splashed all over screens everywhere. Those are the reasons some of the film's depictions will put new realities into the minds of young people. Embed new values into their psyches.

And the fact that we're writing in the oppressor's tongue is certainly telling. But I see it another way, too: our ancestors *survived*. They adapted and did what they had to do to keep the flame alive. We could not be here if each and every single ancestor before us had not survived long enough to birth and sustain us—to pass their progeny into safety so that we could exist... and continue the fight.

Racism and colonization have been destructive, devastating forces, to be sure, but so have patriarchy and misogyny. So to me, it still comes down to ideas and values. This film focused on greed and capitalism as motivating forces behind the plundering of Pandora. Most of the discussion around the film has been around race and imperialism. Absolutely valid. Yet, those same forces of greed and capitalism have been at work in other ways, on a global level, for eons. In India, for instance, women are still, *today*, being burned for being "witches" and in what are often referred to as "dowry deaths." In the case of witch accusations, the women are not being burned by outsiders, and they are not being disconnected from their rituals and traditions. They are killed by people they know, sometimes have known their entire lives, for what they *own*. Victims are usually property-owning women who have chosen to remain single; or, in the case of dowry deaths, young brides who haven't brought enough of a dowry to their new home. What happens to their property when they are killed? The same thing that happened to Jews when they were gassed and to Palestinians when they were forced out of their homes and to women all over Europe who were burned and tortured. It's all about a landgrab, ownership, plundering of resources...greed.

The way I see it, much of the devastation we've seen on a global level, from wiping out hundreds and thousands of women through sanctioned religious executions (both historically and today) to wiping out entire populations during slavery and colonization, often boils down to greed and fear—and capitalism, which has allowed that greed to run rampant and has been fuelled by fear. This was one of the main successes of the film for me, the fact that it tied together issues of environmentalism, patriarchy, race, gender, imperialism...all connected with the thread of greed and corruption.

Also, film, television, magazines, and mainstream media are powerful creators of psychology. They are shapers of vision, culture, ideology, for good or for ill. And I guess I was so exhilarated because (besides the fact that I had very *low* expectations of the film) here were representations of the "other" in ways I could get down with. *Avatar* had all the cheesiness and Hollywood crap in it, absolutely. And for those of us who actively live and breathe the struggle day in and day out, it was not revolutionary by any means. But for the mainstream, I think *Avatar* was definitely quite radical. It was a film that the masses would watch and absorb and it would stick in their psyches, and it wasn't the utter shit we're used to seeing out there—at least not completely.

IZ: No, it wasn't. And at the same time it was—in terms of it being a big budget Cameron production with all the perks (I just bought my son a Na'Vi action figure).

I definitely agree that our ancestors survived, and to my mind, it couldn't have happened any other way. Much like the humans needed to become avatars so they could survive within Pandora's atmosphere, indigenous people could not totally be annihilated for a number of reasons (or else there'd be no fascination with all things voodoo or yoga and curry in the case of you and me as a Haitian and Indian). For me, *Avatar* was a reminder of what has been destroyed. We're here and we overcame, but at what cost? With the spectacular imagery, the foliage and the fauna, I was given a glimpse into some of the magic of our indigenous cultures, and there certainly was magic. It allowed me to romanticize about the breadth and depth of our ancestors' way of life.

In fact, just weeks after I saw *Avatar*, Haiti was hit with the worst earthquake in its history. At the time, I was working on a novel about the indigenous people of what is now Haiti and the Dominican Republic—the Taino and Arawak. I saw many parallels between the film's female lead, Na'vi princess Neytiri, and the legendary Taino queen, Anacaona (Neytiri was played by Dominican-born Zoe Saldana).

In Haitian Vodou, there is something called *Poto Mitan* that is very similar to Pandora's Tree of Souls. The phrase translates literally to "center pole," and this center pole is where the ancestors and spirits reside. The Tree of Souls was the actual physical manifestation of the Na'Vi spirituality. This is what resonated so deeply with me in the movie—spirituality was not just an idea, but was the very backbone of the people's environment. The Na'Vi were physically connected to the animals, the trees, and each other.

Indeed the earthquake brought massive destruction to an already crippled island. However, it is the smaller scale attacks by people like Pat Robertson and those opposed to Haiti's longtime Vodou tradition that are bringing the country to its knees. Haiti, during the time of the earthquake, was our little Pandora and the world responded with genuine compassion. But *Avatar's* RDA (Resources Development Administration, the single largest non-government organization-NGO-operating out of Pandora) is alive and well and is much like the NGOs and politically corrupt local and foreign leaders in Haiti. Yes, *Avatar* was a great movie, but unless the metaphors are connected to our larger world, it will only continue to be just that—a great movie.

NM: Well, I'm certainly glad I went to see it, despite all I'd read and heard—and I am really glad I ended up going to the panel! WisCon would be the only place I could stand to have a conversation about a film like *Avatar*. I particularly enjoyed the after-panel conversations, as well. I got to chat with a couple of panelists, and it seems to me everyone left with lots to think about. It also seems that most people went into the panel thinking they "knew" where they stood on the film but came out with more complexities to consider.

Racial Identity and Writing — Part Six

edited by Eileen Gunn

> **Do you think writers should specifically try
> to write outside their own cultural or racial
> background? Why or why not?
> Should writers stick to what they know best —
> whatever that is — and seek to connect with
> the readers and draw them in? Is there a third
> possibility?**

Claire Light: Yes: try, and keep trying, trying to stretch oneself. All writers should always be trying to stretch themselves in myriad ways. No, writers should never stick to what they know best. They should *start out* writing about what they know best and then move outward, in a search pattern. There are lots of possibilities for ambitious minds.

Nick Mamatas: Writers should be socially aware radical individualists. All elements of trade and traffic, from endeavoring specifically to write a story that'll finally impress Campbell/Dozois/ Williams/Datlow/van Gelder/whomever, to feeling a need to fulfill the mythical and Faustian "contract with the reader," to writing an epic because its "hot," or ethnic because its "in," or whatever your agent says to for the sake of her own bottom line, should be fought against with all one's might in the production of one's work. Once the words are on the page, however, a writer needs to own every syllable and take whatever lumps are forthcoming from the public, and that includes critiques of race depictions, cultural appropriation, etc.

Gavin Grant: Hard question. When I read a novel written in another country, I often want that writer to write about their own culture and racial background. If they write about something else (a Taiwanese writer writing about US immigrants), would I enjoy that level of fictioneering or would I be annoyed at them for not writing about their own culture? I don't know. The only "should" I can use here is that writers should write interesting stories.

Yoon Ha Lee: I would hesitate to tell any individual writer to write outside their cultural/racial background if that wasn't something they already wanted to try. But in general, I would be happier to see more sf/f that doesn't always tread the same well-worn paths. As a reader, I want to feel that writers care about readers who aren't just white (like me!), to question the default. I don't expect that every writer will do this, but it would be encouraging to see more doing so. I'll give you an example: although I've really enjoyed Naomi Novik's Temeraire novels, one of the things that made it difficult for me to connect to the second book in the series, which takes place in China, was that there seemed to be this implicit assumption that the reader was going to be on the British side. Or possibly the French side; I do realize it's Napoleonic warfare with dragons. I just couldn't get on board with this assumption. I would rather be rooting for the Chinese than the British. What made this alienating was not so much the specific book, but the fact that I have had similar experiences with other books. The problem is the cumulative experience of This Book Was Not Really Meant for You.

Writing about other cultures is difficult. I lived nine years in Korea and was raised by Korean parents, and I still find it difficult to grapple with the culture, just as I sometimes have trouble with USAn culture. It's hard to get it right. I worry a lot that any Korean readers who really know the culture will look at my writing and find things that I've gotten grievously wrong. But the only thing to do for it is accept that you're going to screw up sometimes, probably a lot, and own up to your mistakes, and keep trying, because the end goals—affirming that others' (and Others') experiences are important, connecting to other ways of seeing and doing things—are worth it.

Mark Rich: I have no idea what others should do. I barely know what I should do. I sometimes think, with some regret, of the one time I attempted an outwardly Japanese-American character in a short story. The story itself seems fine. It appeared in *Analog*, at least. The character fails to come alive for me, however. I blew it. Most Japanese-Americans of my generation think in ways other than the way I made this character think (I think), even though I wrote him that way. So have I been rushing to my typewriter to jot down scenes involving more J-A characters? Hell, no.

On the other hand, the attitudes that shaped me include racial-cultural ones from both sides. They shape the fiction, too. I have no choice but to write outwards, from within the person that I am, even while constantly taking in the influences of all the people whom I am not.

Sometimes it happens, in writing about characters whom I clearly am not, that I discover a little more about the one I am. Which may supply your answer.

Deb Taber: I definitely think writers should attempt to write outside their own backgrounds if it is appropriate for the story, but they must attempt to portray the characters and experiences outside their backgrounds as whole beings or circumstances, not clichés. The world is not made up of only one type of person, so to give their writing scope and a sense of realism, writers must include more than one viewpoint and character set, whether that means a variety of races, genders, and socio-economic backgrounds, or a set of wholly alien beings. Writing what you *don't* know is a large part of science fiction, and I believe it is the writer's responsibility to educate himself or herself in ways of doing this credibly and with respect. This doesn't mean that every short story should appear as an affirmative-action statement; it just means that stretching your own understanding of the world around you leads to richer storytelling.

As an editor, it saddens me to see good books with well-told stories that fall flat, either because all characters seem to come from the same background, or because race is used merely to distinguish minor characters from each other (i.e., a black man, an Asian woman, the Latino waiter, etc.). My personal preference, as both a writer and a reader, is to keep physical descriptions to a minimum (whether racial or not) and let the character's race, status, or other background details show through in the attitudes, speech patterns, and actions. I think this leads to more thoughtful and respectful multicultural writing, rather than the afore-mentioned affirmative-action story.

Amal El-Mohtar: I think writers should tell the stories they are moved to tell, but not use "telling a story" as an excuse for laziness when it comes to representation or discussion of social issues. I also think writers should challenge themselves and write things that are difficult for them but not for the sake of the challenge alone. These are not mutually exclusive propositions.

I think there's a false dichotomy set up between writers writing what they know and writing outside of their own cultural or racial background. At Readercon last year, Nalo Hopkinson said beautiful things about writing people whose language, appearance, and culture are unfamiliar to us, but what stayed with me most was her saying that we are more alike than we are different. She said that people who speak different languages will nevertheless know what it's like to bite into a piece of fruit. I think that if you write from those similarities outwards, if you seek what you do understand and use that as a fulcrum from which to move towards what you don't understand, you're probably on the right track. It doesn't mean you won't get things wrong, and it doesn't mean you'll be immune from criticism, but take that on board and learn to do better.

Andrea Hairston: I'll quote Senghor again: "I feel the Other, I dance the Other, therefore I am." I write to discover. I also do research. I work that dance with the Other so that I can tell a story. I find my own self doing that dance. It's hard, risky, dangerous, sacred work. Following Gregory Bateson's usage, the sacred is at the nexus of the rational and the irrational, the linear and the nonlinear, the indicative and the subjunctive. Sacred is being and seeming, is metaphor, simile, parable. Objective and subjective, the sacred is the bridge/threshold/edge of consciousness and unconsciousness. Artists are technicians of the sacred—the creators of the fantasy we call reality. I owe it to myself and to whomever I write about to honor the sacred task by challenging myself fully when writing. Writing is a form of knowing. I wish to share that process with readers. I learn and evolve as I go. That's the joy of it.

Ben Rosenbaum: Writers should feel whatever they feel called to do, but it's impossible to avoid writing about the Other. It's good to stretch, and it's good to do your research as best you can, to be responsible and honest about charged topics, and to take risks, make mistakes, and deal with your mistakes responsibly.

Julia Starkey: I disagree with the premises of this question.

I will always write about people different from me, unless I only write about 35-year-old, mixed-race, queer, fat women who have one parent born outside the US and who are also the youngest of two children. This question also presumes that a homogeneous world is both plausible and compelling. Even an artificially created society composed solely of WisCon members would not be homogenous.

I also have issues with the idea that a similarity of racial or ethnic background is what causes readers to connect with a story. One big problem I have is that this concept reinforces the normality of whiteness. I think it also functions to punish authors who are people of color. The presumption is their stories won't have broad appeal, and therefore it doesn't make sense to publish or promote them.

I also have a problem with the idea of "writing what you know," since that is a vague idea that is used to excuse lazy writing and lack of research. I mean, we're all human beings, so does that mean we "know" or understand all other human beings? If an author can write about aliens, telepathic dragons, or 700 year old vampires, it doesn't really make sense that they can't figure out how to understand a person of another race or culture.

I don't want to say it is easy to write about people who are different from you. It's definitely easier to fall back on stereotyping or to ignore their existence. However, that is inexcusably lazy writing, in my opinion. The same libraries and bookstores where I get my speculative fiction can also provide me with a wide array of information about people who are not like me. I may not be able to find every detail about every culture, but I can at least get started with understanding.

I also think authors need to remember that no one gets their book perfect on the first try. The editing process may include revising a character's motivation or adding details that solidify how the fictional world works. It's definitely possible for someone to write compelling, believable stories that are not based in their own culture.

I think once one is aware of racial injustice and how that functions in the publishing industry, it becomes difficult to *not* care about the problems of "lily white futures and monochrome myths." See N.K. Jemisin's essay, "No More Lily White Futures and Monochrome Myths," on K. Tempest Bradford's blog, The Angry Black Woman. (You can Google it.) The question of "writing what you know" would be less of a concern if there were more books by and about people of color.

[Thanks to K. Joyce Tsai, Marta S. Rivera Monclova, Kelly Mulligan, and Tanya D. for helping me explore this topic. J.S.]

Restarting *Clockwork Game*:

A Self-Examination of White Privilege Through an Ongoing Work

by Jane Irwin

When I began writing and drawing *Clockwork Game,* I didn't intend to write a book about Orientalism. I wanted to dramatize a true proto-steampunk story about an inventor, a mountebank, a chess-master, and a medical doctor, and how the same piece of "technology" affected each of them as the Industrial Revolution evolved from concept into reality. Unfortunately for my graphic novel, its subject matter—Wolfgang von Kempelen's Automaton Chess-player, popularly known as "The Turk—" demanded a much more rigorous analysis than it received in the light-hearted romp I'd initially written.

A powerful cultural and political symbol from its very origin, the automaton consisted of a figure dressed as a Turkish man, complete with turban, fur-lined robes, and curled slippers, seated behind a cabinet with a chess set laid out on its finely-crafted lid. In game after game it defeated all opponents, only losing a handful of times throughout its eighty-four-year existence. When I began adapting its history, I understood that I should be careful with my portrayal of the automaton itself, to avoid making it into a bigger caricature than it already was, but during the process of telling the story, I suddenly found this solution insufficient, at best.

My imperfect understanding of the subject matter stemmed from a combination of cultural ignorance and lack of research, or rather, a blinkered focus on only one kind of research. After reading through the first hundred or so essays in RaceFail09, I realized that while I'd spent hours looking up clothing and wigs and scientific discoveries of the day,

I'd devoted almost no time at all to the politics of the era, politics clearly visible to a sizable portion of my audience, but previously invisible to me. I'd been so hung up on examining the Uncanny Valley and seeing the automaton only in terms of man versus machine that I'd completely failed to address the equally large issue of how 18th century Europeans chose to depict and interact with The Mysterious Other. I'd also made a conscious decision to leave out the automaton's relationship to Joice Heth, a black woman once owned and displayed as a sideshow by P.T. Barnum, for fear of taking the story too far off course. The more essays I read, the more glaring these omissions became, as did the privilege behind them. The story I set out to write suddenly felt hollow and disingenuous, naïve.

Under ordinary circumstances, rewriting a manuscript would be a simple matter: just start again from the beginning. But *Clockwork Game* was a webcomic with over fifty pages of completed art online. I knew I couldn't make the necessary changes with the story still in progress, so I put the comic on hiatus while I began a rewrite. I started by re-inter-

rogating all the modern texts I'd read during my initial research phase: none of the three most popular and readily available histories, including one written by a New York Times bestselling author, devoted more than a few lean paragraphs to the automaton's position in the political landscape of its time. Additionally, only one of these three texts contained any information about Joice Heth. Why were these particular portions of its story being so studiously ignored? Was discussing its Orientalist origins or its racist counterparts in stagecraft so difficult that any mention would destroy the narrative? I hoped not, because I was unwilling to continue *Clockwork Game* without such discussion.

Further research turned up all sorts of information, including several texts willing to grapple with the automaton's political history, and the life and death of Joice Heth; it was all there, if only I chose to look for it. After months of reading and thinking, of compiling ideas and throwing them out, I wrote another draft of the script. I sought out an editor with experience in a similar field and delivered the draft: it still wasn't complete enough, and I admit that I acted poorly in response to the editor's critique that the automaton still lacked a sufficient perspective of its own. Returning to the (literal) drawing board filled me with dread and despair, and it was a long time before another draft emerged, this time with an entirely new character: Dr. Yusuf bin Ibrahim.

Dr. bin Ibrahim is a fictitious character heavily based on a real person, Dr. Ibrahim Ben Ali, who came to America after narrowly escaping the Second Russo-Turkish War. Dr. Ben Ali lived in both Liverpool and Philadelphia during the automaton's career, but not at the same time it visited either of those cities. Though there is no explicit evidence that anyone of Turkish descent ever actually saw the automaton play, there must have been at least one if not several during that eighty-year span, and Dr. bin Ibrahim represents that viewpoint. His character not only allows me to conversationally discuss the Orientalism inherent in the automaton, but to bring in even more fascinating history: the story of Al-Jazari's Elephant Clock, a fully-functional water-clock that kept time for the pre-Ottoman Turks in 1205, nearly 600 years before von Kempelen built his more famous *bagatelle* (its obscurity is hopefully short-lived, as an enormous working replica of the Elephant Clock is currently touring across Europe, Turkey, and America with the amazing "1001 Inventions" installation).[1]

These changes to the script, however reassuring, did nothing to address the other Othering going on in the script: the fate of Joice Heth, a former slave and the next-door-neighbor "exhibit" to the automaton. Heth's agency was severely limited by her age, her physical disability, and her position as property of P.T. Barnum, but thanks to the suggestions of my second editor, Nisi Shawl, I was able to turn what was initially a brief conversation between Heth and her female caretaker into a silent, background-image subplot that gave agency and dignity to both women without derailing the story. These additions may even grant the script a technical pass on the Johnson Test, an analog of the Bechdel Test, created by author Alaya Dawn Johnson, which states that:

"1. [The work] has to have two POC in it

2. who talk to each other

3. about something other than a white person."[2]

Despite this progress, I was reluctant to contribute to this anthology because I don't feel that these changes to my script are particularly laudable. I'm still appalled that it took me as long as it did to realize how much I'd missed, with no one to blame for my ignorance but myself.

However, in light of my own initial unwillingness to grapple with the ugly side of the literature and history I hold dear, an outline of my mistakes and eventual path to a different version of *Clockwork Game* may hopefully serve as a reference for other white writers faced with a similar quandary. RaceFail09 inspired me to examine how my race and upbringing, and the blind spots that came with them, affected my perception. While frequently uncomfortable, I feel that confronting my white privilege both made the story stronger and increased my skill as a writer, though that decision must, of course, be left to the reader. My reward for beginning that process — it's only just beginning, after all — is restarting *Clockwork Game* with a story that finally feels complete.

Endnotes

1.   For more information on the touring 1001 Inventions installation
      visit http://www.1001inventions.com/; to watch an animation of
      the way the Elephant Clock worked, visit http://www.youtube.com/
      watch?v=SflvgXhzu7c.

2.   Johnson, Alaya Dawn. "The Bechdel Test and Race in Popular Fiction."
      The Angry Black Woman. 1 September 2009. Retrieved January 21, 2011.
      http://theangryblackwoman.com/2009/09/01/the-bechdel-test-and-
      race-in-popular-fiction/

Excerpts from *Clockwork Game*

by Jane Irwin

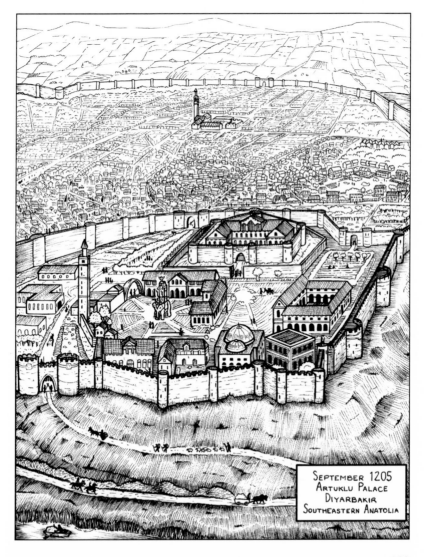

September 1205
Artuklu Palace
Diyarbakir
Southeastern Anatolia

Courtesy of Jane Irwin

WisCon 34 Guest of Honor Speech

by Nnedi Okorafor

I've been spouting off a lot in the last year. *District 9* and its problematic portrayal of Nigerians was like a Pandora's Box.

Today, I just want to tell stories. And I want to explain myself a bit, too.

This past semester I taught a course in Popular Literature (I'm a creative writing and literature professor at Chicago State University). For this class, I chose the theme of "setting." My secret diabolical plan was to mess with my students' heads until they questioned what "normal" was. I wanted to really stimulate their imaginations.

When we started out, only one of my students knew what a graphic novel was and none of them read speculative fiction. The perfect group with whom to launch my plan.

I had them read *Persepolis, Aya, The Gunslinger, Things Fall Apart, Krik Krak,* and *The Hole.*

By the end of the semester:

- They'd seen the conflict and history of Iran from a young girl's perspective

- They'd seen a part of Africa that was not riddled with disease, war, or famine.

- They'd watched an ancient man and his ancient gun kill an entire town.

- They'd witnessed an Igbo community fall apart.

- They'd gone deep into Haiti.

- And they'd dabbled in technologically-advanced Voodoo.

After all that, the final book was my novel, *The Shadow Speaker*. By this time, I figured this book would be a piece of cake for them. They'd been exposed to all sorts of creativity, my flavor of it couldn't possibly be jarring, right? I wouldn't need to explain a thing.

My students (who were predominately black) really enjoyed *The Shadow Speaker*. On the day we discussed the book, they were especially eager to hear about how I went about writing it; little did I understand why they were so interested.

That day, I explained my Nigerian-American background, my obsession with the Sahara Desert, my fascination with the apocalypse, fear of sudden change, love of creatures, beasts and monsters, my questioning the necessity of violence, my need to portray an Africa of the future, my constant creation of strong unique active female characters, blah blah blah.

As I talked, I realized everyone was kind of frowning. They'd look at each other and smile or quietly laugh with each other. They seemed more and more perplexed.

Finally, one of my students raised her hand and said, "You want me to be honest?"

"Of course," I said. Now I was frowning.

"Well, we all thought you were just sitting around smoking weed and thinking things like, 'Yeah, a living sandstorm, that would be cool. A sword-wielding Muslim woman with two husbands? Let's throw that in, too.'"

Then another student chimed in, nodding vigorously, "Yeah, I mean, I assumed with the dreadlocks and all, that you were definitely... 'smoking the peace pipe.'"

Another student added, "And you're always so...happy."

Pause

I felt sweaty and irritated. It had never crossed my mind that my students would interpret things this way. Not after all we'd read and discussed and processed.

This whole experience heightened my already present need to explain myself.

So let's clear the air...*pun intended*.

- ◆ I am not a Rasta.

- ◆ I don't smoke (*anything*).

- ◆ I don't drink.

- ◆ My only "vice" is chocolate, which from what I know does not have any hallucinatory side effects.

Though maybe it does as it is the food of the gods, goddesses, spirits, and demons...tasting of smooth goddessly paradise and produced from demonly evil.

(If you know anything about child slavery in the cocoa fields of the Ivory Coast, which are supported by huge companies like Nestlé and Hershey, you know what I'm talking about.)

But I digress.

I've always been like this...creative. I was born this way. No hallucinatory substances needed. Who needs drugs and alcohol when you have life?

I didn't start writing fiction until I was 20, and I didn't have anyone to introduce me to science fiction or fantasy. I was eventually drawn to it. I was a very imaginative child.

I had my entire second grade class believing that they were genetically part rabbit and part human (I chose rabbits because I could flare my nostrils just like a rabbit). And I had them also believing that just beyond the school grounds was not the highway but another world where there were wild horses, giant butterflies, and of course millions of rabbits (not the cartoonish bipedal kind, but regular rabbits).

I was sure the red thorny bush on the playground was infected with a demon. I told my classmates to never ever let it prick them, or their eyes would turn red and they'd forget their names. And they believed me. I could be quite persuasive.

During my first trip to Nigeria, when I was seven, I realized that there were grasshoppers that clicked when they flew and sneaky spiders that were thin as paper. My imagination thrived there.

When I learned that sow beetles were not insects at all, but really crustaceans, I walked around grinning. We had a lot of them in our basement, and I loved the idea that there were these creatures related to crabs and lobsters lurking in the house.

In second grade, I created a butterfly out of many sheets of construction paper. I spent all of my free time that day working on it. When I finished, I excitedly sat on it and waited. And waited, and waited, and waited. When it didn't come to life and politely offer to fly me into the sky, I was seriously pissed.

My imagination and my interest in living things was what kept the more dangerous monsters at bay. While I was looking up the kingdoms, phylums, classes, orders, families, genuses, and species of the grasshoppers and frogs in the back yard, I was too distracted to pay much attention to the racism in my neighborhood.

In 2004, I wrote this bit of nonfiction for an anthology on race and childhood called *Under Her Skin*. My essay was called, "Running Girl," and it really summed up much of my childhood. Here's a bit from it:

> When I was young, I was always running. And so this Wednesday in 1982 was much like any other day back then.
>
> I was running fast; close at the heels of my two older sisters, Ngozi and Ifeoma. I was breathing hard because I was terrified.
>
> Uniform homes flew by as I ran. Red brown white bricks, white painted wood, fences that were recently placed around houses and backyards, and white Ford Mustangs and Datsuns with black speed stripes, and once in a while a weedy empty lot.
>
> During more peaceful moments, when I wasn't being chased by a group of young racists, I would traipse around in these places looking for what I could find.
>
> The light green bulbous spittlebugs were easy to locate. They lived in a dollop of saliva-like fluid. When they grew up, they'd be green and sometimes rainbow-colored leafhoppers. Lovely. My favorite creatures were the chunky yellow, black, and red fat-butted grasshoppers and florescent green katydids.
>
> However at the moment, I wasn't at peace. I wasn't where I wanted to be at all. It was the middle of summer, eighty-five degrees, not a cloud in the sky. The sun shone brightly on exactly what was happening underneath it. I wore pink shorts, a rose-colored shirt, and dirty white Keds. My legs and arms

were like toothpicks, and people at school called me Palm Tree, Nnedi Spaghetti, and Daddy Long Legs, among other, less savory things.

"We're gonna get you, niggers!"

Ifeoma was ten, Ngozi was nine, and I was eight. All of the kids chasing us were in high school. The three of us had come around a corner, on our way home from the park when we met the group of white kids. My sisters and I had frozen as we stared back at the seven, eight kids. The moment was a stalemate of realization. All of our schedules were about to be modified.

The white kids were no longer going to talk shit to each other for the next fifteen minutes about why the Scorpions rocked, and my sisters and I were no longer going to take the short way home. Without a word, the three of us took off. Ifeoma leading, then Ngozi, and then me. Our shiny gherri curls dripped oil and sweat into our eyes.

Now, as we ran, I was sure in my stride, so I snuck a glance back. We would outrun them, though we were much younger.

My sisters and I took a wrong turn and we were eventually cornered in front of a fence. It was a decisive moment. These kids chased us all the time but they had never *caught* us.

We still talk about what happened next. The three of us acted at the same time. Ife and Ngozi turned and hopped the fence. I, on the other hand, had a more imaginative plan. I ran forward, dove through one of the taller boy's legs and took off. Our two-tiered response was so confusing to those kids that they just stood there, indecisive of which way to go.

When I look back, it makes complete sense that I'd write what my uncle in Nigeria with his thick accent calls, "dis ting....eh, eh, magic stories, science fiction." And it makes complete sense that I wound up here.

This is my fifth year at WisCon.

Writers, readers, editors, agents, creators, destroyers, thinkers, movers, shakers, troublemakers, I love coming here. I'm comfortable here. So is my daughter Anyaugo. I almost didn't bring her but when

I told her that she wouldn't be going, the look on her face could have caused a rift in the time continuum.

There's energy here, and my daughter and I are both attracted to that.

One more story: Weeks ago, I received an ecstatic email from an Igbo guy in Nigeria. He was one of those people born dada (with dreadlocks — *Zahrah the Windseeker* is based on this concept). This guy had just read *Zahrah*. He said that all his life he'd been stigmatized for being born dada. He said my novel had blown his mind. He said it had never crossed his mind that being dada could be a positive thing. Mission accomplished.

There is a Nigerian proverb that says "With a little seed of imagination you can grow a field full of hope." There is nothing like a good story.

Nnedi Okorafor gives her Guest of Honor speech at WisCon 34.

WisCon 34 Guest of Honor Speech

by Mary Anne Mohanraj

I've always wanted to be a hero. When I was a kid, I loved science fiction and fantasy for many reasons, but mostly because I identified with the hero of the story. With *A Wrinkle in Time*, I was Meg; with *The Dark is Rising*, I was young Will. In *The Once and Future King*, I was the boy Wart, who would someday become Arthur Pendragon, create the Round Table, and bring the light of justice and chivalry to a dark world.

My favorite hero is Frodo, because he is so ordinary. As Le Guin says in *The Language of the Night*, Frodo is one of us, someone who has no fancy skills, no magic powers. What he has is a group of strangers telling him that he's the one they need—he's the only one who can take on this incredibly difficult task and thereby save the world. That moment in the Council of Elrond, when it's clear the task is too big, too hard, too awful, and Frodo, knowing this, speaks up softly and says, "I will take the ring, though I do not know the way,"—that chokes me up, every time. Growing up, I wanted to be that brave, if the call ever came to me.

In the stories, there's always that moment when a stranger appears to the young hero, when the wise old man shows up at your doorstep with a flaming sword and says to you—*we need you, you're the chosen one, you're the only one who can save us*. I grew up waiting for that call, waiting for someone to open my door, and reach out his hand to me. The call could come at any moment; that doorway could open to another world. Sometimes, walking alone down a street, seeing a shadowed door, I would step into the shadow, just in case. It was never a magic door, but I kept hoping. I *keep* hoping.

My family is traditional and conservative. My parents had an arranged marriage, and expected the same for me. I wasn't allowed to date, or even go to school dances. So when I started fooling around with boys in high school, I did it in secret. I hid under the basement stairs, terrified that my sisters might come downstairs and catch us, with some boy's hands under my shirt, unhooking my bra. It took some courage, but teenage hormones helped. It took more courage to come out to my parents about it, to tell them that I was actually dating, and worse, dating white boys. I waited until I was safely thousands of miles away at college to tell them, and it was still terrifying.

I had years of screaming fights with my parents—at various points, they threatened to send me to a convent in Sri Lanka, or told me that I was raising their high blood pressure, and that I was going to give them heart attacks. My mother cried herself to sleep at night, and at one particularly bad point, stopped speaking to me for six months. But I held firm.

Some might call that selfishness, or ingratitude, or cruelty. Some did. But I thought then, and I still think, that it was important to draw that line in the sand, to say that I owned my own body, and I was the one who would decide who could touch it, and when, and how. I wouldn't have labeled it feminism at the time, but now I would call it a feminist move, to find the courage to stand up for that right over my own body, against my parents, against the whole culture they came from, a culture that they were trying to impose on me.

I found that once I stood up to them about my right to date (and by implication, to have sex), it became easier to break other taboos. I started dating women too. And I eventually stopped trying to be monogamous. Monogamy had never felt right for me, but it took me some time to be brave enough to admit it. I started writing about sex, and putting what I wrote online, and that was perhaps the most frightening of all. My parents got a call from a relative in England, saying, "Do you know what your daughter is putting on the internet?" They responded, "What's the internet?" And were horrified by the answer.

All through my twenties, I was a sex activist. I went to college campuses and talked to South Asian students about sex. I wrote erotica and published it online and in print. I had strangers write me hate mail, or send me unsolicited underwear to my unpublished real address, or call me up at three in the morning and ask where they could go to get sex. Sometimes I felt threatened, under attack. Sometimes I would cry. I wanted to stop, to just give up, so many times. But I believed the work

I was doing was important, and sometimes people would take the time to tell me how much they valued it, and that gave me the strength to keep going.

I did that work for ten years. By the time I turned thirty, I felt like I had said most of what I wanted to say about sex. I started writing around race and ethnicity, which carried a different set of dangers. I was writing, often obliquely, about the war back home in Sri Lanka, about the Tamil Tigers and the ongoing ethnic conflict. I struggled with two different kinds of fear. The first was an immediate physical fear that if I said the wrong thing about the Tigers, or the Sinhalese government, someone might actually come after me. I might be in physical danger, or even killed, as others had been. It didn't seem likely in America, but it was possible. Mostly, I dealt with that fear by trying not to think about it.

I worried much more about the second problem—that I might get things wrong. That if I, a Sri Lankan-American far removed from the conflict, wrote something about the war and got it wrong, by simple virtue of my living in America and writing in English, my words might be taken as true, might influence people or policy in dangerous ways. That fear almost paralyzed me, almost kept me from writing, and I still struggle with it every time I write about Sri Lanka.

I do my research; I try to learn as much as I can so I can get things right, as right as I can. I keep writing, but my words are often more cautious, less bold than I would like them to be. I second-guess myself constantly—I say things, and then retract them, soften them. I hide the political stories in fantasy worlds that bear only a passing resemblance to Sri Lanka. But at least I keep trying, which is a kind of courage, I think. It's better than not speaking at all.

When I was thirty-five, my partner Kevin and I decided to try to have a child. I found myself assaulted by a whole new set of fears. I had recently developed fibroids, and I was terrified that I had waited too long, that I would be infertile and unable to have a child. Then, once I became pregnant, I went through much of the pregnancy darkly convinced that something would go wrong. The child would be ill, injured, would die—over and over during that pregnancy I became convinced that she had, in fact died, and that I just didn't know it yet. I was afraid of the childbirth too, afraid I wouldn't be strong enough to handle the pain. I almost couldn't believe it when it was all over and I finally had a healthy baby girl. It didn't seem real.

Interestingly, I'm not sure I'd call any of that experience me being courageous. Because once I was actually pregnant, I was just in it for the ride. My job was to endure whatever came, hopes and fears and everything else. Whether I embraced the experience or not, this pregnancy was happening, this baby was coming, and my courage or lack of it was irrelevant, sidelined by the sheer biology of it all.

Sometimes there's nothing we can do in the face of difficulty but grit our teeth and try to endure.

But what I found much harder in the end, what has been the hardest challenge of my life, is actually parenting. As it turns out, I hate babies. I didn't love my daughter Kavya at first—I didn't love her for months. She was a screaming, weeping, inexplicable mess that wouldn't let me sleep and made me more than a little psychotic. I would get so angry during those first few months with her, it was all I could do to keep myself from shaking or hitting her—anything, if she would just please shut up. I'm not normally an angry person. I don't have a lot of practice in fighting back rage. I found it tremendously hard not to resort to violence. If Kevin hadn't been right there in the trenches with me, doing his fifty percent and maybe a bit more, I'm not sure I would have made it.

It got easier when she got older and I could talk to her, reason with her. I wasn't nearly as tempted to hit. But I still had, and still have, a very hard time putting her needs first, ahead of my own desires. I had almost twenty years as an adult before I had her, twenty years of being the center of my own universe. I'd been partnered with Kevin for almost that entire time, but he was an adult, able to stand up for himself. It's very different, knowing that this small person is dependent on me, that she relies on me to be strong, to endure whatever misery she's putting me through. Not hitting, is perhaps the minimum standard for decent parenting, but some days, meeting that minimum standard isn't easy for me. Being a decent parent doesn't feel particularly fun, and certainly not heroic. And yet, I think in a way, it is. Doing the right thing, even when it's hard and you don't want to. That's a big part of heroism.

Now, you could say that I asked for it, that I chose to have a child, and that maybe I shouldn't get extra credit for that bare minimum of decent parenting. All I can say in response is that I'm guessing you haven't been woken up for the eighteenth time by a baby who screams and just will not go to sleep, no matter how many lullabies you sing to it, or how long you jiggle it in your aching arms. I'm not sure any parent-to-be has any real understanding of what they're signing up for—I'm not sure they *can*. That's just the nature of the beast. Some find babies easy, I hear. For me, they've been torture, and it has taken all my willpower to do the right thing.

To be fair, I must have found some parts of parenting pretty good, because we did decide to have a second one. Once we got past the worst of the baby stage, Kavya actually got kind of fun. Sometimes, your heroism is rewarded.

That's what I tell myself now, with our second child, Anand, still refusing to sleep. Sometimes, a glimmer of hope is all that gets you through the night.

I want to talk about the kind of heroic work that so many of you in this room are engaged in—the work of social justice, combating sexism, racism, ageism, ableism, transphobia, homophobia, etc. and so on. In my own life, that mostly plays out in two arenas these days, gender and race. In the feminist realm, my battles against sexism are pretty quiet, and mostly involve things like making Kevin sit down with me and talk about the distribution of household labor. Even though he's a sensitive new age guy who wants and tries to be fair, who is philosophically committed to a 50/50 egalitarian household, he's still a man raised in a certain time and place. There are some kinds of labor that he wasn't taught to value, some kinds of labor that he just doesn't see. It's scary, forcing those conversations that might put our relationship at risk, but it's also fighting for justice, for myself, and so that our children will see and absorb a different model of shared labor.

It helps more than I can say that Kevin is committed to fighting sexism as an ally. It's astonished me, realizing how even for an enlightened, feminist man, it can be so hard on a daily basis to consciously give up those privileges. It's not so bad when life is easy, when time and money are hanging ripe for the picking. But when life starts squeezing, and every moment of free time becomes precious, it takes an effort of will to hold back from taking more than your share. Especially when society is pushing us both, so hard, towards the sexist path, it takes both effort and sacrifice on his part to fight to preserve my freedom and rights. Whether it's being willing to follow my career, or splitting the childcare, or making sure I get a room of my own to work—I barely have the energy to fight society for my rights as a woman. I don't think I could do it if I had to fight my partner too.

※

Heroism isn't necessarily big things. It's being brave and doing what you're scared to do, doing what's hard for you—what might be easy for someone else. We all have to calibrate this for ourselves, calculate the difficulty of the task, our own weariness, and how much we can bear. It can be hard to see clearly what the heroic action is.

Right now, for me, heroism is writing about Sri Lanka and the war, even if I have to touch on it oh-so-lightly in mainstream fiction or memoir, or code it in the description of a fantasy world. It's putting my children's needs first when they actually need me, no matter how much I resent it—and sometimes putting my own needs first, over their desires, no matter how much society shakes its disapproving head. Heroism is arguing with Kevin about housework. It's valuing my work and taking care of myself. It's doing what I know is right, even when it's hard, and relying on allies to help.

It's resting when I am too tired to go on, so I can survive to fight another day.

※

When I got the call from Debbie Notkin asking me to be Guest of Honor at WisCon, my initial response was, "Are you sure you want me?" Debbie started laughing, but I was serious. After all, I'd never published a single book of science fiction or fantasy; I didn't feel like I'd earned the Guest of Honor title. All through this convention, while people have been so kindly congratulating me on the role, there's been a small voice in the back of my head saying I don't deserve it, and if they only knew how little I'd done, they'd be furious, and take the title away.

That's impostor syndrome, that sense that you're not good enough, not as good as everyone else, that you don't deserve the recognition that you receive. It's widespread — my professors in grad school told me they felt it, even after tenure. My doctor sisters feel it too, and my freshman students as they write their first college papers. Almost everyone I've asked has experienced impostor syndrome at one point or another — and it's a dangerous feeling, because it gets in your way. It makes you think that you're not good enough to be a hero, you're not the one to do the job that needs doing. You minimize your own talents, your skills and strength and accomplishments. You sit back, and let someone else do the work, and tell yourself that they'd do a better job anyway.

When RaceFail happened last year, I ended up spending most of a week on John Scalzi's blog *Whatever*, trying my best to do some social justice work, teaching Racism 101. It was hard, and scary, but important too, for the health and sanity of a community I have grown to love over the decade I've been coming to WisCon. Many people gave me advice and help during that week — other writers, editors, readers, and my sweetie, Jed Hartman. In particular, I want to acknowledge Kevin's help during that week. This isn't even his community, but it was his financial and childcare and emotional support (as I occasionally burst into tears reading some of the mean, angry comments on Scalzi's blog) that got me through. That's a different kind of heroism, doing what he could to make my own work possible. He couldn't do the job for me, but he held me up while I did it. He's home taking care of our children now, not sleeping, making it possible for me to be here.

In the SF/F community in the past few years, there have been a series of incidents around social justice — feminist issues, race issues, more. I think more are coming. I expect that along with RaceFail, we're going to see TransFail, AgeismFail, DisabilityFail. And that's scary, but it's also good. We're at a critical moment, a shifting of the social norms, and we are the ones defining what the new norms will be, what is and is not okay in our community.

This is a time for heroes. This is a time when we need *many* heroes. It's too much for one person, or a few people, to do all by themselves. You may think that these aren't your battles, but if you love these books, the people in this room, this community, then these issues affect you. These social justice struggles matter. And we need your help.

It can be frightening, speaking up against a friend, or someone you perceive as a powerful editor. It's hard, speaking up against your entire community. It's particularly hard when you're not even sure you're in the right. It's upsetting when you discover that sometimes you are the one at fault, and you are the one who has done damage with your words, your actions, damage that you're not sure you can heal. It can be humiliating to realize just how wrong you were, and it can take courage to admit your wrong-headedness out loud. But just because it's frightening and hard, doing this work, doesn't mean that you can't do it.

I think you can.

I think we need to fight through those expectations, fight against the idea either in our own heads or imposed by others that we aren't competent to do the job. We have the right as writers, as readers, as human beings, to engage with any idea we want to. Maybe it isn't your direct lived experience—maybe you have to make something of an imaginative leap to get there. Maybe you have to do research to keep from getting things wrong. You're going to get things wrong. But you can't let the fear of being told that you're wrong, or not good enough, stop you from trying.

Because here is one truth I know—

The world *is* in terrible danger. *You* have been chosen, you are needed, you are each and every one of you the only one who can save it, if you will just be brave enough. And it will be hard. But heroism isn't about not being afraid. It is about being afraid, and doing the work anyway. Fighting for what you know is right. And I promise you this—for every time you stand up for the cause you believe in, every time you break down one of the walls of fear to speak out, you will emerge stronger and braver on the other side.

I'm a literature professor now, and a fiction writer. As I grew up, I never stopped loving science fiction and fantasy; I never stopped loving stories, in part because good stories reveal character, and character reveals the fundamental truths of the human heart. It takes clear sight and courage to look at what is revealed inside us, dark and bright, and show that openly to the world. One of my favorite writers, Dorothy Allison, said that the best writing comes when we are terrified, and we write the truth anyway. So I am asking you to look clearly at the world around you, its beauty and its terrible pain and injustice. I'm asking you to take up that flaming sword, because it is here; I am standing on your doorstep, and I am calling you. You *can* be brave enough, you can be a hero.

The best of it is that if you lead the way, others will follow.

Deep in our hearts, I believe we all want to be heroes.

Mary Anne Mohanraj gives her Guest of Honor speech at WisCon 34.

Telling Our Stories: Looking Back on the Book Panel on *"Why Are All the Black Kids Sitting Together in the Cafeteria?" And Other Conversations About Race* by Beverly Daniel Tatum, PhD

by LaShawn M. Wanak

I moderated the panel mentioned in this essay's title (considered the panel with the longest name to date) at Wiscon34. By doing so I changed a man's life.

Not bad considering that was my first full WisCon. I had attended the previous year, but only for one day. I'd had so much fun, though, that I decided to try my hand at a panel in 2010. I had picked up a free copy of the book *"Why Are All the Black Kids Sitting Together in the Cafeteria?"* some time ago, so I figured this would be a good chance for me to read the book. I signed up to be on the panel based on it.

Imagine my surprise when I learned that not only had I made it on the panel, but I was also going to moderate it. To give you an idea what I was in for, here is the sum of my panel experience before WisCon 34:

1) Sitting with Tobias Buckell and Karen Babich on a mock race panel "White People in SF" at 2010's OddCon X, also held in Madison.

2) Doing an "Internet Publishing Panel" roundtable at this same convention.

And here is the sum of my experience of moderating panels:

1)

As you may have guessed, I was a *teeny-weeny* bit concerned.

A few days after the panel was officially set to go, the panelists received an email that challenged the terminology in Tatum's book. The individual who sent that email had also questioned the creation of POC safer spaces at WisCon; most of his criticism boiled down to: "What if the whites decided to have a safe place that was 'whites only.' Would that be considered racist?"

Race is such a hot-button topic. To discuss it rationally requires a certain amount of finesse and sensitivity, and a determination not to interject your own bias into the conversation. At a loss about what to do, I fretted, planned, sent questions to my co-panelists, plotted out a course of discussion, scrapped that, plotted out another course, then scrapped that too. When the time for the panel came, I gave up and decided to do what I was best at.

I told stories.

Tatum's book is an excellent discourse on the nature of race from an African American perspective. It gives a thoughtful analysis of how African Americans see themselves, how they live day-by-day with the knowledge that they are not considered the "norm" but always "the other." It was a very good critique of how race is viewed in general, but I felt it was lacking in several ways. First, I'm not academically-minded, so it took a while for me to cut through the jargon to get to the meat of the book. Second, some of the examples Tatum gives felt too general, too cookie-cutter, for me to relate to them.

For instance, Tatum describes an adolescent black teen who was called "Oreo" by her black peers, but never really fit in with her white peers either. It wasn't until she joined a gospel choir that she found a black community where she was able to fit in and feel accepted. Tatum concludes that black parents should "provide ongoing opportunities for their children to connect with other Black peers even if that means traveling outside the community they live in" (p. 69).

When I was twelve, my mother had me join a Bible study group for black preteens that met in a different neighborhood. I got to know them pretty well, but one girl in particular constantly teased me about how I talked "proper" and was always reading. One day, she took me aside and said, "You know, a lot of other kids gonna start calling you Oreo and stuff. You need to start acting blacker if you want real friends." I shied away from her after that, and once study had ended for that year I didn't go back. Tatum's recommendation didn't work for me because, well, I was a geek. And in the black neighborhood where I lived in, being a geek made you an outcast.

When I reached high school, for the first time I met white males who were just as nerdy as I was, so naturally I hung out with them. This did make for some interesting relationships; I went through the frustration Tatum outlines in the book of being attracted to white males who did not share my feelings. My first boyfriend was a white freshman who scribbled a note to me on how we made such a cute Oreo couple (we broke up after that). But I also went out with white males who didn't see me as an exotic girlfriend, but who genuinely liked me for who I was; in fact, one of those relationships culminated in a marriage that's been going strong for twelve years now.

Gradually, the racial make-up of my group of friends transitioned from black to white. Still, I went through a crisis of identity when I realized that part of me longed to really be an accepted member of the African American community. In my first year of college, I went with the few people on my dorm floor to a black fraternity step show, a synchronized performance that's part cheerleading, part drill exercises, and part stomping. While I loved the show, I couldn't connect with the people around me. They talked about things that I had little interest in: rappers, the latest dance fad, clothes, hairstyles. I just smiled and nodded, pretending to know what they were talking about. Standing there, among talking, laughing people, I felt very alone.

In contrast, later that year, I found an on-campus bible study made up mainly of whites, with a couple of Asians sprinkled in for good measure. We got into a discussion about Tolkien and C.S. Lewis, as well as other fantasy writers who weren't Christian but wrestled with theological issues. Now *this* I cared about. I easily became part of the group and liked it so much, when I left college to work fulltime, I attended meetings of another group of the same organization on a different campus.

I grew extremely comfortable being around white people, but I occasionally still felt the difference, particularly when I went to a church or a rock concert where there was no brown face to be seen but mine. While I did not have any overt racism happen to me, I became keenly aware that people saw me as the "token black person." So I had resigned myself to spending most of my life as an outsider, not really connecting with any race.

It wasn't until I started writing professionally that I found I wasn't alone. When I moved to Madison two years ago, I fell in with a book club who encouraged me to come to WisCon, where I found an abundance of people *just like me*: in mind, in heart, and in skin color.

For the first time in my life, I was *not* the token black woman in a group. There were other African Americans out there, men and women who also wrote fantasy and science fiction, who loved anime, rock music, and all things geeky. Who talked about their favorite fanvids instead of the latest gangsta rap videos. Who did not shy away from hot topics such as privilege and RaceFail, and then turned around to gush about Serenity (while simultaneous praising Josh Whedon and bashing him).

These were my people. These were the group I had been looking for all my life. These were the kids I wanted to sit together with in the cafeteria.

Between myself and the other members of the panel—Isabel Schechter, Luke McGuff, and Saira—we had diverse upbringings; some of this matched what was in the book, some did not. We shared our stories and in doing that we were able to touch on something that was not explored in Tatum's book—the nature of fandom for people of color. The other panelists had their own life experiences, their own tales, but we all agreed on one thing—WisCon was a place where we could feel at home. We could get together and talk and laugh and have a good time, and we could also get together to share our fears and concerns. These were safe places for us, places where we could express our opinions without fears of being misunderstood or shot down, but also places where we could enjoy something that had always been denied to us for, a place where we could *belong*.

Only about ten people showed up to listen to the panel, but that's okay. It made for a rich time of sharing, not just among the panelists, but also among the audience members. At the end, a man rose and thanked us for sharing our stories, saying "I now understand the need for safer places for people of color." Later, I learned that not only was this the person who'd sent the email I mentioned earlier criticizing that idea, but that people had been trying for *years* to get him to understand the need for what he was so set against. He had always been resistant to the need until our panel. And once I recovered from my dead faint (the one caused by learning of his presence), I realized that in simply telling our stories, we were able to change this person's view about safer spaces. We did it! Us!

We can go on and on about rhetoric and logic and terminology. We can spout out terms like "privilege" and "racism" until we're blue in the face. But such words don't have an impact unless we have a way to tie them to story. It is through us telling our stories, over and over again, that we can help people different from us put themselves into our shoes and experience what we've experienced. Exactly how that process affects someone is up to each person, but one can never hear a story and come away unaffected.

Now you know my story.

And I hope that guy does campaign for white people to have their own safer space at WisCon. According to Tatum's book, that's a great idea.

Bibliography

Tatum, Beverly Daniel. (1997). *"Why Are All the Black Kids Sitting Together in the Cafeteria?" And Other Conversations About Race.* New York: Basic Books.

Contributor Biographies

Known as "raanve" everywhere there's an internet, **Jess Adams** is an academic, writer, and fan from southwest Ohio. She completed her bachelor's in creative writing at Miami University in Oxford, Ohio, and is currently a graduate student in composition and rhetoric at Wright State University. Her work has appeared in *Elysian Fiction* and *Cincinnati CityBeat*. She has also self-published her own zine, *Letterbox*. Jess lives in Dayton, Ohio, with her husband, a dog, and three cats. The fourth cat is just a foster—honest.

Terry Bisson explores the mysteries of the human heart in his stories and novels. He also writes science fiction. He lives in California.

Maurice Broaddus is the author of the novel series The Knights of Breton Court (Angry Robot). His dark fiction has been published in numerous magazines, anthologies, and websites, most recently in *Dark Dreams II* and *III*, *Apex Magazine*, *Black Static*, and *Weird Tales Magazine*. He is the coeditor of the *Dark Faith* anthology (Apex Books). Visit his website at www.MauriceBroaddus.com.

Tanya C. DePass is a 37-year-old sci-fi fan who was raised on a diet of original series Star Trek, Battlestar Galactica, and written sci-fi as soon as she was old enough to hold a book on her own. She's a lifelong Chicagoan and is mum to one grey-and-black tabby, and will eventually grow up, whatever that means.

Amal El-Mohtar is an Ottawa-born child of the Mediterranean currently pursuing a PhD in English Literature at the Cornwall campus of the University of Exeter. She is the author of *The Honey Month*, a collection of poetry and prose written to the taste of 28 different kinds of honey, and co-edits *Goblin Fruit*, an online quarterly dedicated to fantastical poetry, with Jessica P. Wick. Her stories and poems have appeared in many print and online venues, and are forthcoming in Ann and Jeff VanderMeer's *The Thackeray T. Lambshead Cabinet of Curiosities* and Ellen Kushner and Holly Black's *Welcome to Bordertown.* "The Green Book," a short story which appeared in the Arab/Muslim issue of *Apex Magazine,* has been nominated for the Nebula award.

Oussama Ajaj El-Mohtar, father of poet Amal El-Mohtar, is the Lebanese Canadian translator of her poem "Song for an Ancient City." His work has appeared in *Fikr* magazine's January 2010 issue.

Candra K. Gill is a lifelong sf fan, a longtime WisCon attendee, a bookbinder, and a lover of power chords. She serves on the Carl Brandon Society Steering Committee and is a staffer with the Organization for Transformative Works. She is currently pursuing a master's degree specializing in Human-Computer Interaction.

Greer Gilman's book *Cloud & Ashes: Three Winter's Tales* won the 2010 James Tiptree, Jr. Award in concert with Fumi Yoshinaga's *Ōoku: The Inner Chambers, Volume 1.* Like Gilman's earlier novel *Moonwise, Cloud & Ashes* is set in a Northern mythscape, linguistically intricate. Her Cloudish tales have also won a World Fantasy Award and a Crawford Award, and have been nominated for the Nebula and Mythopoeic Fantasy awards. Besides her two books, she has published other short work, poetry, and criticism. Her essay on "The Languages of the Fantastic" will appear in *The Cambridge Companion to Modern Fantasy Literature.* Gilman has been a Guest of Honor at the International Conference for the Fantastic in the Arts and at Readercon. She holds a Master of Arts from Cambridge University and is a graduate of Wellesley College. A sometime forensic librarian at Harvard, she lives in Cambridge, Massachusetts.

Jaymee Goh is a writer of speculative fiction and scholar/blogger of critical theory. She has contributed to *Tor.com, Racialicious.com*, the *Apex Book Company Blog, Beyond Victoriana.com*, and *Steampunk II: Reloaded* (Tachyon Publications, 2010). Her fiction has been published in *Expanded Horizons* and *Crossed Genres,* and she has co-written an essay on steampunk fashion and race for *Fashion Talks* (SUNY Press, 2012). She graduated from Saint Mary's University in Halifax, Nova Scotia, with an Honors degree in English and is currently working on an MA in Cultural Studies and Critical Theory at McMaster University in Hamilton, Ontario. Her blog (www.jhameia.com) explores issues of marginalization and culture, and she analyses steampunk literature from a postcolonial perspective at *Silver Goggles* (http://silver-goggles.blogspot.com).

Gavin J. Grant runs Small Beer Press and since 1996 has published and edited (with Kelly Link) *Lady Churchill's Rosebud Wristlet.* He has written for *Strange Horizons*, the *Los Angeles Times*, and *Time Out New York*, among other periodicals. Originally from Scotland, Grant now lives with Link and their daughter, Ursula, in Boston.

Short-story writer **Eileen Gunn** is author of the collection *Stable Strategies and Others* (Tachyon Publications, 2004) and coeditor of *The WisCon Chronicles, Volume Two* (Aqueduct Press, 2008). She has received the Nebula and the Sense of Gender awards, been nominated for the Hugo, Philip K. Dick, and World Fantasy awards, and shortlisted for the Tiptree. She was editor/publisher of the *Infinite Matrix* webzine and in the dead of night can hear it stomping around in the attic.

Andrea Hairston is the author of *Redwood and Wildfire* (Aqueduct, 2011) and *Mindscape* (Aqueduct, 2006), which was shortlisted for the Phillip K. Dick and Tiptree Awards, and a winner of the Carl Brandon Parallax Award.

MJ Hardman, Professor of Linguistics and Anthropology at the University of Florida, has been researching the Jaqi languages of Peru, Bolivia, and Chile for the last half century plus. She also writes grammars, cultural studies, and bilingual education materials, as well as participates actively in the implementation of language preservation. She is now putting a lot of the resulting material online: the first part as a free-access, self-taught course in Aymara (http://aymara.ufl.edu/); the second part as pioneering programming for Jaqaru/Kawki recordings from 50 years of fieldwork, with full-text analysis. She teaches language and gender/culture/violence as well as, on occasion, Linguistics and Science Fiction. She is about to publish an online book on making the invisible visible (cited in "The Russ Categories").

Hardman came to sf very, very late, mostly dragged there by her children. She has attended WisCon every year since the first Tiptree Award—with recent exceptions because of health—usually accompanied by her husband, Dr. Dimas Bautista of the Jaqi people of Perú. Both Hardman and Bautista were involved in the founding of the Carl Brandon Society, and they now belong to the CBS's Circle of Elders. They will be celebrating their golden anniversary in 2012. They live in Florida and in Peru, both on Peru's coast and in the Andes.

Jane Irwin is the artist and writer of the Vögelein series of graphic novels, the first of which was listed among *Booklist*'s Top Ten Graphic Novels for Youth in 2003. She is currently serializing *Clockwork Game*, a dramatization of the history behind the world's first chess-playing automaton, at www.clockworkgame.com.

Sf/f critic **Mari Kotani** has served as vice president of the Science Fiction and Fantasy Writers of Japan and as chair of the Women Writers Committee of the Japan PEN Club, which has promoted the movement of anti-textual harassment. Her first book, *Techno-Gynesis: The Political Unconscious of Feminist Science Fiction* (Tokyo: Keiso Publishers, 1994) won the 15th Japan SF Award, the Japanese Nebula. As one of the active members of The Japanese Association of Gender Fantasy and Science Fiction, she helped found the Sense of Gender Award, the Japanese equivalent of the James Tiptree, Jr. Award. She has also served as an advisor to the organizers of TOKON 10, a venerable Japanese science fiction convention presented by feminists in 2010 for the first time in its nearly 50 years of existence. A frequent presence at WisCons past, she may possibly also attend WisCon 35.

Yoon Ha Lee lives in California with her family and occasionally writes Asian-flavored sf/f. Her stories have appeared in *The Magazine of*

Fantasy and Science Fiction, Clarkesworld, Beneath Ceaseless Skies, and
Lightspeed.

Claire Light is inimitably based in Oakland, bloggin', writin' fiction,
organizin' creative writin' programs, and generally havin' a good ol'
time.

Nick Mamatas is the author of several novels, including *Sensation*
(PM Press), and dozens of short stories. With Ellen Datlow he
edited *Haunted Legends,* and five days a week edits Japanese sf/f in
translation for Haikasoru.

Neesha Meminger's debut YA novel, *Shine, Coconut Moon,* was listed
as a Smithsonian Notable Book in 2009 and was one of the top one
hundred books for teens as rated by the New York Public Library's *Stuff
for the Teen Age.* She also writes paranormal erotic romance under a
pen name and has several titles out involving lusty shapeshifters.

Mary Anne Mohanraj is the author of *Bodies in Motion* (HarperCollins,
2005) and nine other titles. *Bodies in Motion* was a finalist for the Asian
American Book Awards and has been translated into six languages.
Mohanraj founded the World Fantasy Award-winning and Hugo
Award-nominated magazine *Strange Horizons.* She was Guest of Honor
at WisCon 34, received a Breaking Barriers Award from the Chicago
Foundation for Women for her work in Asian American arts organizing,
and won an Illinois Arts Council Fellowship. Mohanraj is Clinical
Assistant Professor of fiction and literature and Associate Coordinator
of Asian and Asian American Studies at University of Illinois at Chicago,
and serves as Executive Director of both DesiLit (www.desilit.org) and
the Speculative Literature Foundation (www.speclit.org). Recent sf/f
publications include "Talking to Elephants" at *Abyss & Apex* and "Jump
Space" at *Thought Experiments.* She lives in a creaky old Victorian
in Oak Park, just outside Chicago, with her partner, Kevin, two small
children, and a sweet dog. She's currently working on a YA fantasy
trilogy in which youngsters from our world travel to a magical island
very similar to ancient Sri Lanka.

Nancy Jane Moore writes everything from flash fiction to novels. Her novella *Changeling* (2004) is available from Aqueduct Press and her collection *Conscientious Inconsistencies* (2008) from PS Publishing. She is a founding member of the online writer's co-operative Book View Café, where she published a series of 51 flash fictions in its first year of operation. Her fiction has appeared in magazines ranging from *The National Law Journal* to *Lady Churchill's Rosebud Wristlet*, various online venues, numerous print anthologies, and several ebook anthologies from Book View Café. In addition to writing, Moore studies the martial art of Aikido, in which she holds a fourth degree black belt. After living for many years in Washington, DC, she returned to her native Texas in 2008 and now lives in Austin.

Librarian **Zola Mumford** is Curator of the Langston Hughes African American Film Festival, a program of the Langston Hughes Performing Arts Center in Seattle, Washington. Her background includes arts event management, film and TV production, historical research, and preservation work with film and print materials in university and private film and art archives. She holds Washington state librarian certification and is a member of the American Library Association, the Association of College and Research Librarians, the Society of American Archivists, and the Carl Brandon Society.

Kate Nepveu was born in South Korea and raised in New England. She now lives in upstate New York where she is practicing law, raising a family, and (in her copious free time) writing at her Dreamwidth account (kate_nepveu), a booklog (steelypips.org/weblog), and *Tor. com*, where she has just concluded rereading *The Lord of the Rings* one chapter a time.

James Ng (pronounced "Ing") was born in Hong Kong, where he spent most of his childhood drawing monsters and robots, making his own elaborate cardboard toys, and playing soccer. Ever since he has been on the move between Hong Kong, Vancouver, Chicago, and New York. His travels have greatly influenced him, allowing him to combine Eastern and Western cultures in his artwork.

Currently James is enjoying the freedom of being a freelance concept artist and illustrator. After spending a sunny summer in Vancouver and traveling to London and then to New York for an award show and exhibition, he returned to Hong Kong to plan for his next trip. One day he hopes to start a design company with some friends, and maybe even direct a movie featuring all his monsters and robots. James would love to hear your comments and criticism regarding his artwork. Feel free to drop him an email at jamesngart@gmail.com. All messages will be answered!

Nnedi Okorafor is a novelist known for her complex characters and for weaving Nigerian cultures and settings into science fiction narratives. Her YA novels include *Akata Witch* (Penguin Books, 2010); *Zahrah the Windseeker* (Houghton Mifflin, 2005), winner of the Wole Soyinka Prize for African Literature; *The Shadow Speaker* (Hyperion, 2007), winner of the Carl Brandon Parallax Award; and *Long Juju Man* (Macmillan, 2009), winner of the Macmillan Prize for Africa. Her first adult novel, *Who Fears Death* (Daw, 2010), was chosen as a Best Book of 2010 by Amazon.com, *Publishers Weekly*, and *School Library Journal*. Okorafor is a professor at Chicago State University. Visit her at nnedi.com.

Mark Rich is the author of *C. M. Kornbluth: The Life and Works of a Science Fiction Visionary*, a biography/critical evaluation of Kornbluth, published in March 2010 by McFarland. He lives in the Wisconsin Coulee region.

Benjamin Rosenbaum's stories have appeared in *Strange Horizons*, *Nature*, *The Magazine of Fantasy and Science Fiction*, *Asimov's*, *Harper's*, and *McSweeney's*, been nominated for the Hugo, Nebula, BSFA, Locus, and Sturgeon awards, and translated into sixteen languages. You can find them at http://benjaminrosenbaum.com and http://theantking. com. He lives near Basel, Switzerland with his wife and two children.

Nisi Shawl's Aqueduct Press story collection *Filter House*, lauded by Ursula K. Le Guin as "superb" and by Samuel R. Delany as "simply amazing," won the 2008 James Tiptree, Jr. Award and was nominated for two 2009 World Fantasy Awards. Shawl is also the coauthor of *Writing the Other: A Practical Approach* (Aqueduct, 2005), a guide to developing characters of varying racial, religious, and sexual backgrounds; it received a James Tiptree, Jr. Special Mention the year after it was published. Shawl is one of the founding members of the Carl Brandon Society, a nonprofit dedicated to supporting the representation of people of color in the fantastic genres. She edits reviews for *The Cascadia Subduction Zone*, Aqueduct Press's quarterly literary review, and is coeditor with Dr. Rebecca Holden of *Strange Matings: Octavia E. Butler, Feminism, Science Fiction, and African American Voices*, forthcoming from Seven Stories. Shawl's speaking engagements include presentations at Duke University, Stanford University, and Smith College. In May 2011 she is WisCon 35's Guest of Honor. She blogs at http://nisi-la.livejournal.com.

Vandana Singh is an Indian writer currently living in the Boston area, where she teaches physics at Framingham State University. She was born and raised in New Delhi, where she acquired an early interest in science, the environment, and social justice issues. Her experience of being an alien from the Third World has driven much of her fiction, which has been published in magazines and anthologies such as *Strange Horizons*, *So Long Been Dreaming*, and *Clockwork Phoenix*, and reprinted in a number of Year's Bests. Her first collection, *The Woman Who Thought She was a Planet* (Zubaan/Penguin India), came out in India in 2008, and she has two novellas out from Aqueduct Press: *Of Love and Other Monsters* (2007)and *Distances* (2008), a Tiptree Honor Book and winner of the Carl Brandon Parallax Award. She is also the author of the ALA Notable children's book *Younguncle Comes to Town* (Viking/Penguin, 2006).
Her website is at http://users.rcn.com/singhvan/.

Julia Starkey is a geeky, mixed-race, fat, queer, librarian-in-training. She lives in a big city with two cats and lots of books. Julia is still working on not over-committing herself.

Deb Taber is the senior book editor with Apex Publishing, an award-winning speculative fiction small press. Her writing has been published in *Fantasy Magazine, Shadowed Realms, Apex Digest*, and various anthologies, and is forthcoming in the literary anthology *Art From Art* (Modernist Press). Learn more about her work at www.inkfuscate.com.

Maria Velazquez is a doctoral student at the University of Maryland, College Park. Her research interests include constructions of race, class, gender, and sexuality in contemporary media, as well as community-building and technology. She serves on the board of Lifting Voices, a District of Columbia-based nonprofit that helps young people in DC discover the power of creative writing. She blogs for *The Hathor Legacy* (www.thehathorlegacy.com), a feminist pop culture blog, and recently received the Winnemore Dissertation Fellowship from the Maryland Institute for Technology in the Humanities. She has also received a fellowship from the Consortium on Race, Gender, and Ethnicity's Interdisciplinary Scholars Program. Maria is a Ron Brown Scholar and an alumna of Smith College. Her dissertation project examines the use of the body as a component in community building, paying particular attention to the Bellydancers of Color Association, the anti-racist blogosphere, and Red Light Center, an adults' only virtual world. When she is not quietly fomenting academic dissent or playing Echo Bazaar, she writes poetry and prose.

Chicagoan **LaShawn M. Wanak** lives in Madison, Wisconsin, with her husband, her son, and her in-laws. Surprisingly, she is still sane. Her short fiction has appeared in *Ideomancer, Expanded Horizons*, and *Daybreak Magazine*. Visit her at *The Cafe in the Woods* (tbonecafe. wordpress.com), another writer's blog *In Touch with Yours Truly*.

Heidi Waterhouse is a professional technical writer and an amateur mother, poet, knitter, and critic of usability flaws. She lives in the Pacifc Northwest and spends a lot of time trying to figure out if everyone else feels like they're faking it, too.

Alberto Yáñez is a writer of fantasies, bad poetry, and essays on justice, agency and art, and the absurdity of life in San Francisco. He also likes to take pictures. His approach to photography is documentarian, but he hopes that every picture tells a story. Nora Jemisin once called him the "chronicler of the revolution" in jest, and he aspires to live up to the title. He's grateful for the generosity of others in allowing him to record and share these moments.

Fumi Yoshinaga, an acclaimed and award-winning *mangaka*, was born in Tokyo, Japan, in 1971. She attended the prestigious Keio University in Tokyo. *The Moon and the Sandals*, first of her many full-length graphic works, appeared as a serial in the Japanese magazine *Hanaoto* in 1994. In 2005 her novel *Ōoku: The Inner Chambers, Volume 1* received a Sense of Gender Award from The Japanese Association of Gender Fantasy and Science Fiction, and in 2010 its US edition received the James Tiptree, Jr. Award in concert with Greer Gilman's *Cloud & Ashes*. Her favorite operas are by Mozart.

Doselle Young is a Los Angeles-based author and graphic novelist. He has written several stories for DC Comics, including his own twelve-volume series, The Monarchy. His fiction appears in the anthology *The Darker Mask* (Tor, August 2008).

Ibi Zoboi was born in Haiti, and she's been published online, in literary journals and in anthologies, including the award-winning *Dark Matter: Reading the Bones*. A graduate of the Clarion West Writers Workshop, she drew from Haitian mythology and folklore to complete a teen fantasy novel.

Praise for The WisCon Chronicles series

"What I admire most about these WisCon Chronicles is not just the collection of intelligent thought, and the best example of documenting the convention experience I have ever seen, but the acknowledgement of the bad parts as well as the good—the exposure of privilege, of negative as well as positive reactions to the discussions, and the willingness to shine a bright torch on all the grey areas, for the purpose of greater and more constructive conversation."

~ Tansy Rayner Roberts, *As If*, August 2009

The WisCon Chronicles: Vol. 1
Edited by L. Timmel Duchamp

The WisCon Chronicles: Vol. 2
Provocative Essays on Feminism, race,
revolution, and the future

Edited by L. Timmel Duchamp
and Eileen Gunn

The WisCon Chronicles: Vol. 3
Carnival of Feminist SF
Edited by Liz Henry

The WisCon Chronicles: Vol. 4
Voices of WisCon
Edited by Sylvia Kelso

(Supported by a grant from the Society for the Furtherance & Study of Fantasy & Science Fiction [SF3].)